Editors
Kim Fields
Sara Connolly

Managing Editor
Ina Massler Levin, M.A.

Illustrator
Howard Cheney

Cover Artist
Courtney Barnes

Art Coordinator
Renée Christine Yates

Art Production Manager
Kevin Barnes

Imaging
Rosa C. See
Nathan P. Rivera

Publisher
Mary D. Smith, M.S. Ed.

W9-CTR-846

NONFICTION READING COMPREHENSION

Informational Reading

Grade 3

Ideal for Test Practice

Includes Standards & Benchmarks

Author

Tracie Heskett, M.Ed.

Teacher Created Resources, Inc.
6421 Industry Way
Westminster, CA 92683
www.teachercreated.com
ISBN-978-1-4206-8863-4
©2007 Teacher Created Resources, Inc.
Made in U.S.A.

Table of Contents

Introduction

Reading comprehension can be practiced and improved in the context of informational reading, as well as in the reading students do in the course of their daily lives. This book presents environmental print in the context of scenes and other print media, along with short stories of explanation. The topics chosen include familiar settings and experiences while at the same time introducing new vocabulary and ideas.

A page of questions follows each story. These questions will provide a child familiarity with different types of test questions. In addition, the practice they provide will help a child develop good testing skills. Questions are written so that they lead a child to focus on what was read. They provide practice for finding the main idea, as well as specific details. They provide practice in deciphering new and unknown vocabulary words. In addition, the questions encourage a child to think beyond the facts. For example, every question set has an analogy question where students are expected to think about the relationship between two things and find a pair of words with the same type of relationship. Other questions provide an opportunity for the child to infer and consider possible consequences relevant to the information provided in the story.

The book is designed so that writing can be incorporated into every lesson. The level of writing will depend on what the teacher desires, as well as the needs of the child.

Lessons in *Nonfiction Reading Comprehension: Informational Reading (Grade 3)* meet and are correlated to the Mid-continent Research for Education and Learning (McREL) standards. They are listed on page 8.

A place for *Nonfiction Reading Comprehension: Informational Reading (Grade 3)* can be found in every classroom or home. It can be a part of daily instruction during time designated for reading or other academic areas as specific topics of study relate to the stories presented. It can be used for both group and individual instruction. Stories can be read with someone or on one's own. *Nonfiction Reading Comprehension: Informational Reading (Grade 3)* can help children improve in multiple areas, including reading, critical thinking, writing, and test-taking.

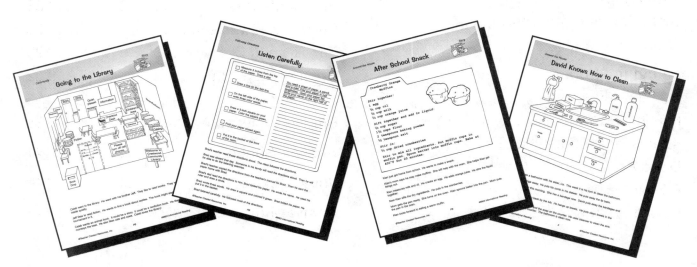

Using This Book

The Stories

Each story in *Nonfiction Reading Comprehension: Informational Reading (Grade 3)* is a separate unit. For this reason, the stories can be (but do not have to be) read in order. A teacher can choose any story that coincides with classroom activity.

Stories can be assigned to be read during reading or other related academic periods. They can be used as classroom work or supplemental material.

Each story contains a scene or sample of environmental print, as well as a short story of explanation. The stories range from 50 to 200 words in length. They are written at the first grade level and have elementary sentence structure.

New Words

Each story includes a list of eight vocabulary words. These words may be used in the short story or the environmental scene. New words may sometimes have an addition of a simple word ending such as *s, ed,* or *ing.* Many of the new words are found in more than one story. Mastery of the new words may not come immediately, but practice articulating, seeing, and writing the words will build a foundation for future learning.

* A teacher may choose to have the children read and repeat the words together as a class.

* While it is true that the majority of the words are defined explicitly or in context in the stories, a teacher may choose to discuss and define the new words before the students begin reading. This will only reinforce word identification and reading vocabulary.

* A teacher may engage the class in an activity where children use the new word in a sentence. Or, the teacher may use the word in two sentences. Only one sentence will use the word correctly. Children will be asked to identify which sentence is correct. For example, one new word is *fix.* The teacher might say,

> "They will fix the movie."

> "She will fix dinner."

* A teacher may also allow children to choose one new word to add to their weekly spelling list. This provides children with an opportunity to feel part of a decision-making process, as well as to gain "ownership" over new words. In addition, practice spelling words reinforces the idea that we can learn to recognize new words across stories because there is consistency in spelling.

* A teacher may choose to have children go through the story after it is read and circle each new word.

Using This Book *(cont.)*

The Writing Link

✻ A teacher may choose to link writing exercises to the stories presented in the book. All writing links reinforce handwriting and spelling skills. Writing links with optional sentence tasks reinforce sentence construction and punctuation.

✻ A teacher may choose to have a child pick one new word from the list of new words and write it. Space for the word write-out is provided in this book. This option may seem simple, but it provides a child with an opportunity to take control. The child is not overwhelmed by the task of the word write-out because the child is choosing the word. It also reinforces word identification. If a teacher has begun to instruct children in cursive writing, the teacher can ask the child to write out the word twice: once in print, and once in cursive.

✻ A teacher may choose to have a child write a complete sentence using one of the new words. The sentences can be formulated together as a class or as individual work. Depending on other classroom work, the teacher may want to remind children about uppercase letters and ending punctuation.

✻ A teacher may require a child to write a sentence after the story questions have been answered. The sentence may or may not contain a new word. The sentence may have one of the following beginnings:

- I learned . . . .
- I thought . . . .
- Did you know . . . ?
- An interesting thing about . . . .

If a teacher decides on this type of sentence formation, he or she may want to show children how they can use words directly from the story to help form their sentences and utilize correct spelling. For example, this is the first paragraph in the selection titled "Field Day."

Today Jamal will go to a field day. Many soccer teams will play. Jamal's team will play three or four other teams. One team will win the final game. That team will be the champions.

Possible sample sentence write-outs:

"I learned that Jamal's team will play more than one team."

"I thought that you could only play one soccer game in a day."

"Did you know champions win the final game?"

"An interesting thing about soccer is that many people play it."

This type of exercise reinforces spelling and sentence structure. It also teaches a child responsibility—a child learns to go back to the story to check the spelling. It also provides elementary report writing skills. Students are taking information from a story source and reporting it in their own sentence construction.

Using This Book *(cont.)*

The Questions

Five questions follow each story. Questions always contain one main-idea, specific-detail, and analogy question.

* The main-idea question pushes a child to focus on the topic of what was read. It allows practice in discerning between answers that are too broad or narrow.

* The specific-detail question requires a child to retrieve or recall a particular fact mentioned in the story. Children gain practice referring back to a source. They also are pushed to think about the structure of the story. Where would this fact most likely be mentioned in the story? What paragraph or part of the scene would most likely contain the fact to be retrieved?

* The analogy question pushes a child to develop reasoning skills. It pairs two words mentioned in the story or scene and asks the child to think about how the words relate to each other. A child is then asked to find an analogous pair. Children are expected to recognize and use analogies in all course readings, written work, and listening. This particular type of question is found on many cognitive-functioning tests.

The remaining two questions are a mixture of vocabulary, inference, identifying what is true or not true, or sequencing questions. Going back and reading the word in context can help answer vocabulary questions. The inference and sequencing questions provide practice for what students will find on standardized tests. They also encourage a child to think beyond the story. They allow a child to think critically about how facts can be interpreted.

The Test Link

Standardized tests have become obligatory in schools throughout our nation and the world. There are certain test-taking skills and strategies that can be developed by using *Nonfiction Reading Comprehension: Informational Reading (Grade 3)*.

* Students can answer questions on the page by filling in the correct bubble, or you may choose to have your students use the provided answer sheet (page 141). Filling in the bubble page allows students to practice responding in a standardized-test format.

* Questions are presented in a mixed-up order, though the main-idea question is always among the first three questions. The analogy question is always one of the last three questions. This mixed-up order provides practice with standardized test formats, where reading comprehension passages often have main-idea questions, but these types of questions are not necessarily placed first.

The Test Link *(cont.)*

✳ A teacher may want to point out to students that often a main-idea question can be used to help a child focus on what the story is about. A teacher may also want to point out that an analogy question can be done any time since it is not crucial to the main focus of the story.

✳ A teacher may want to remind students to read every answer choice. Many children are afraid of not remembering information. Reinforcing this tip helps a child remember that on multiple-choice tests, one is identifying the best answer—not making an answer up.

✳ A teacher may choose to discuss the strategy of eliminating wrong answer choices to find the correct one. Teachers should instruct children that even if they can only eliminate one answer choice, their guess would have a better chance of being correct. A teacher may want to go through several questions to demonstrate this strategy. For example, in the story scene "A Special Evening," there is the question:

---

3. This story is mainly about
   - (A) eating popcorn
   - (B) seeing the neighbor
   - (C) using a remote control
   - (D) reading a book

Although popcorn, the neighbor, and a remote control are mentioned in the story, there is no mention of a book. A child may be able to eliminate that answer choice immediately. A guess at this point has a better chance of being correct than when there were four choices to choose from. A teacher can remind children, too, that there is the option of going back and finding the parts of the story with the words *popcorn, neighbor,* and *remote control* in them. The story refers to *popcorn* and the *neighbor.* In fact, they appear to have equal weight. As one cannot be a better choice than the other, neither one of them can be correct.

Environmental Print

The term *environmental print* refers to the "printed words children see every day in the world around them." These words may be on signs, posters, containers, or buildings. Children read environmental print at home, in the classroom, stores, other places in the community, and outdoors. They also encounter print on a regular basis on directions, maps, and various types of schedules. Children become familiar with the words they see every day and can often read much more than others realize. Practice reading for information in various formats allows children to gain confidence in their reading comprehension and test-taking abilities as they encounter print with which they are already familiar.

Meeting Standards

Listed below are the McREL standards for language arts Level 1 (grades 3–5). All standards and benchmarks are used with permission from McREL.

Copyright 2004 McREL

Mid-continent Research for Education and Learning

2550 S. Parker Road, Suite 500

Aurora, CO 80014

Telephone: (303) 337-0990

Website: *www.mcrel.org/standards-benchmarks*

McREL Standards are in **bold**. Benchmarks are in regular print. All lessons meet the following standards and benchmarks unless noted.

Uses stylistic and rhetorical aspects of writing

- Uses a variety of sentence structures in writing (*All lessons where writing a complete sentence option is followed.*)
- Uses grammatical and mechanical conventions in written compositions
- Writes in cursive (*All lessons where teacher follows the option of writing a sentence using a new word or completion of beginning sentence options in cursive.*)
- Uses conventions of spelling, capitalization, and punctuation in writing compositions (*All lessons where teacher follows option of writing a sentence using a new word or completion of beginning sentence options.*)

Uses the general skills and strategies of the reading process

- Previews text
- Establishes a purpose for reading
- Represents concrete information as explicit mental pictures
- Uses phonetic and structural analysis techniques, syntactic structure, and semantic context to decode unknown words
- Uses a variety of context clues to decode unknown words
- Understands level-appropriate reading vocabulary
- Monitors own reading strategies and makes modifications as needed
- Adjusts speed of reading to suit purpose and difficulty of material
- Understands the author's purpose

Uses reading skills and strategies to understand a variety of informational texts

- Summarizes and paraphrases information in texts
- Uses prior knowledge and experience to understand and respond to new information

Shopping for Dinner

These are new words to practice.
Say each word 10 times.

✳ produce	✳ item
✳ lettuce	✳ fix
✳ each	✳ taco
✳ tortilla	✳ aisle

Choose one new word to write.

_____

- - - - - - - - - - - - - - - - - - - -

_____

Shopping for Dinner

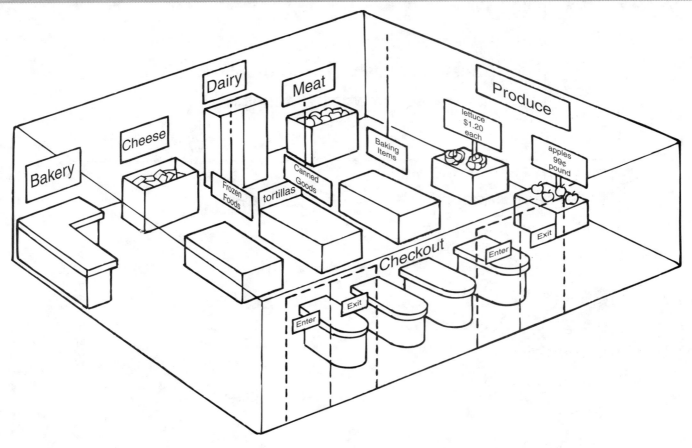

Kala went to the store with her aunt. They will fix dinner for her mom. It is her mom's birthday.

Kala wants to have tacos. They will need meat. They will put cheese on the tacos. They will get lettuce and a tomato.

Kala's aunt looks for tortillas. She finds them at the end of an aisle. Kala says they need a birthday dessert.

Her mom likes apple pizza. Kala gets some apples. Her aunt says they need flour.

They have everything they need now. They buy the food. Kala's mom will like this dinner!

Shopping for Dinner

**Look at the picture on page 10. Read the story.
Use the picture and the story to answer the questions.**

1. Kala puts meat on tacos. Where will she find meat?

   (A) on the left side of the store

   (B) at the back of the store

   (C) right next to frozen foods

   (D) in the front of the store

2. This story is mainly about

   (A) going to the store

   (B) making dinner

   (C) having a birthday

   (D) buying cheese

3. Kala will help fix dinner. She will

   (A) repair something

   (B) decide something

   (C) place something

   (D) prepare something to eat

4. Think about how the word *dairy* relates to *milk*. Which words relate in the same way?

dairy : milk

   (A) produce : lettuce

   (B) enter : exit

   (C) cheese : checkout

   (D) tacos : dinner

5. Kala wants to make apple pizza. She will need flour. Where will she most likely find flour?

   (A) produce

   (B) frozen foods

   (C) baking items

   (D) bakery

Going to the Library

These are new words to practice.
Say each word 10 times.

* library
* information

* magazine
* reference

* fiction
* nonfiction

* drop
* catalog

Choose one new word to write.

_____

- - - - - - - - - - - - - - - - - - -

_____

Going to the Library

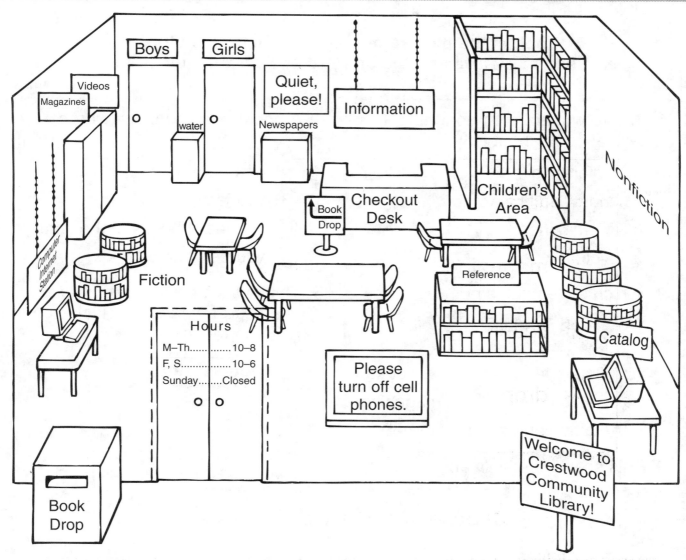

Caleb went to the library. He went with his brother Jeff. They like to read books. They walk inside quietly.

Jeff likes to read fiction. He wants to find a book about castles. The book might also have a tournament in it.

Caleb wants an animal book. It could be a story. It could be a nonfiction book. He likes monkeys the best. He also likes cats and cows. Caleb loves the library!

Going to the Library

**Look at the picture on page 13. Read the story.
Use the picture and the story to answer the questions.**

1. Where would Caleb go to find a factual book about cows?

    (A) reference

    (B) nonfiction

    (C) magazines

    (D) fiction

2. Which statement is not true?

    (A) Caleb can talk on a cell phone.

    (B) Caleb can check out a book.

    (C) Caleb can look at a magazine.

    (D) Caleb can use the Internet.

3. This scene is mainly about

    (A) computers

    (B) a checkout desk

    (C) information

    (D) a library

4. A book *drop* is a place where

    (A) you let books fall on the ground

    (B) you leave words out of a book

    (C) you leave books in the library

    (D) you put a small book

5. Think about how the word *fiction* relates to *nonfiction*. Which words relate in the same way?

fiction : nonfiction

    (A) boys : girls

    (B) library : books

    (C) magazines : newspapers

    (D) computer : Internet

Pizza Party

These are new words to practice.
Say each word 10 times.

✳ perfect   ✳ arcade

✳ topping   ✳ restroom

✳ order   ✳ pepperoni

✳ extra   ✳ token

Choose one new word to write.

_____

– –

_____

Pizza Party

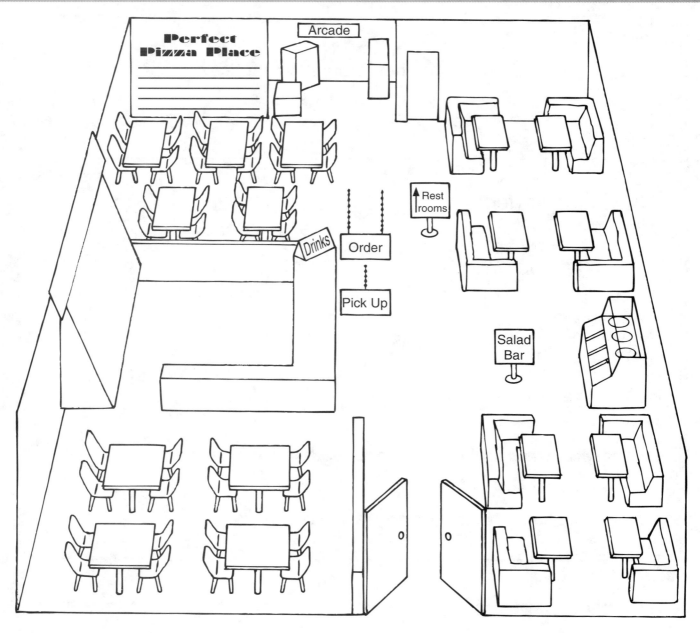

Clark's soccer team had a pizza party. The players on the team went to Perfect Pizza Place. They sat in the back. They could put tables together. The team all sat in a group.

The coach ordered pizza. They got two extra large pizzas. One had pepperoni on it. The other had bacon and pineapple.

Each boy got a drink. They also got tokens. They used the tokens to play games.

16

Pizza Party

**Look at the picture on page 16. Read the story.
Use the picture and the story to answer the questions.**

1. The coach *ordered* pizza. The team

   (A) sold pizza

   (B) told the boys to eat pizza

   (C) got something to eat in a restaurant

   (D) placed the pizza in a line

2. Why did the team put tables together?

   (A) to build a fort

   (B) to sit as a group

   (C) to sweep the floor

   (D) to play a game

3. This story is mainly about

   (A) playing arcade games

   (B) playing soccer

   (C) getting pizza

   (D) being a coach

4. What kind of pizza did the coach order?

   (A) chicken

   (B) small

   (C) cheese

   (D) pepperoni

5. Think about how the word *coach* relates to *players*. Which words relate in the same way?

coach : players

   (A) salad : drink

   (B) teacher : students

   (C) small : large

   (D) restroom : arcade

Fitness Is Fun

These are new words to practice.
Say each word 10 times.

✳ reserve   ✳ racquetball

✳ treadmill   ✳ mark

✳ exercise   ✳ sole

✳ weights   ✳ allow

Choose one new word to write.

_____

- - - - - - - - - - - - - - - - - - - -

_____

Fitness Is Fun

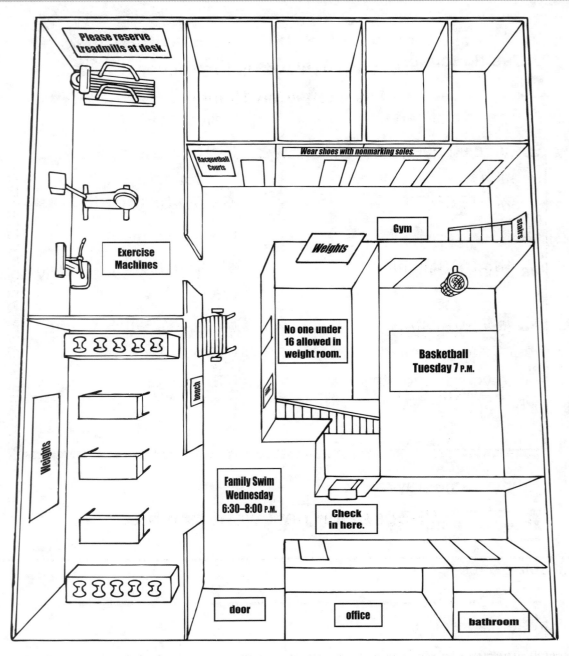

Holly's family joined a health club. They all want to lose weight. They want to work out and be healthy.

The club has exercise machines. Holly likes to walk on the treadmill. Her mom walks, too.

Holly's dad likes to play basketball. He plays with Holly's older sister. She plays well.

They all like to swim. Every week they go to Family Swim.

Fitness Is Fun

**Look at the picture on page 19. Read the story.
Use the picture and the story to answer the questions.**

1. This story is mainly about

   (A) a swimming pool

   (B) a health club

   (C) a gym

   (D) a ball

2. What is a health club? It is a place

   (A) where you exercise

   (B) where you eat salad

   (C) where your friends talk

   (D) with a leader

3. Think about how the word *exercise* relates to *machine*. Which words relate in the same way?

exercise : machine

   (A) sole : shoe

   (B) health : club

   (C) treadmill : weights

   (D) racquetball : basketball

4. Holly's sister is

   (A) good at baseball

   (B) younger

   (C) older

   (D) the same age

5. What does Holly's family do every Wednesday?

   (A) go to Family Swim

   (B) play racquetball

   (C) walk on the treadmill

   (D) eat salad

Going to the Clinic

These are new words to practice.
Say each word 10 times.

✷ clinic	✷ cotton
✷ lab	✷ records
✷ waste	✷ shot
✷ scale	✷ wait

Choose one new word to write.

_____

- -

_____

Going to the Clinic

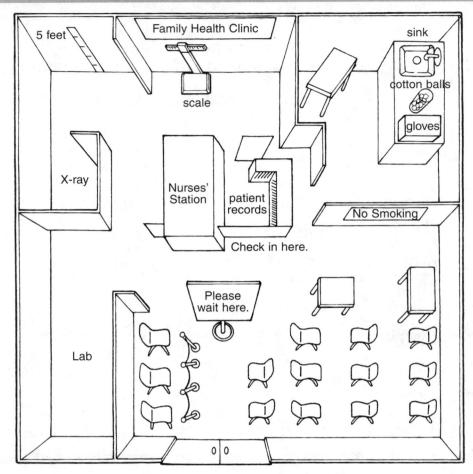

Garrett went to the family health clinic. He got his hand caught in the car door. His mom wants to see if it is broken.

Garrett sat and waited. A nurse called his name. Garrett's mom walked with him.

The nurse checked Garrett's height and weight. He stood next to a wall chart. The nurse measured him. Then Garrett stood on the scale. The nurse made notes on his chart.

She took him to a room. Garrett sat on a table. He saw cotton balls and gloves on the counter next to the sink. The nurses and doctors use those things.

The doctor came in. He checked Garrett's hand. He didn't think it was broken. He told Garrett to have an X-ray to make sure.

The nurse took Garrett to the X-ray room. They took a picture of the bones in Garrett's hand. His hand looked okay.

Garrett could leave. He didn't need a cast on his hand. He didn't want to come back to the clinic for a while.

Going to the Clinic

**Look at the picture on page 22. Read the story.
Use the picture and the story to answer the questions.**

1. What is by the sink?

   Ⓐ patient records

   Ⓑ a scale

   Ⓒ gloves

   Ⓓ a hat

2. This story is mainly about

   Ⓐ getting a shot

   Ⓑ waiting for the nurse

   Ⓒ going to the clinic

   Ⓓ having a cold drink

3. Where could Garrett get help if he was sick?

   Ⓐ the dentist

   Ⓑ the clinic

   Ⓒ the store

   Ⓓ the library

4. Think about how the word *nurse* relates to *clinic*. Which words relate in the same way?

   nurse : clinic

   Ⓐ cotton : ball

   Ⓑ cashier : store

   Ⓒ wait : waste

   Ⓓ health : clinic

5. Garrett sat and waited. He

   Ⓐ asked his mom for help

   Ⓑ served the nurse lunch

   Ⓒ looked forward to seeing the doctor

   Ⓓ did nothing until someone called him

Back to School

These are new words to practice.
Say each word 10 times.

✳ supply	✳ ruler
✳ backpack	✳ glitter
✳ glue	✳ marker
✳ notebook	✳ eraser

Choose one new word to write.

_____

- -

_____

24

Back to School

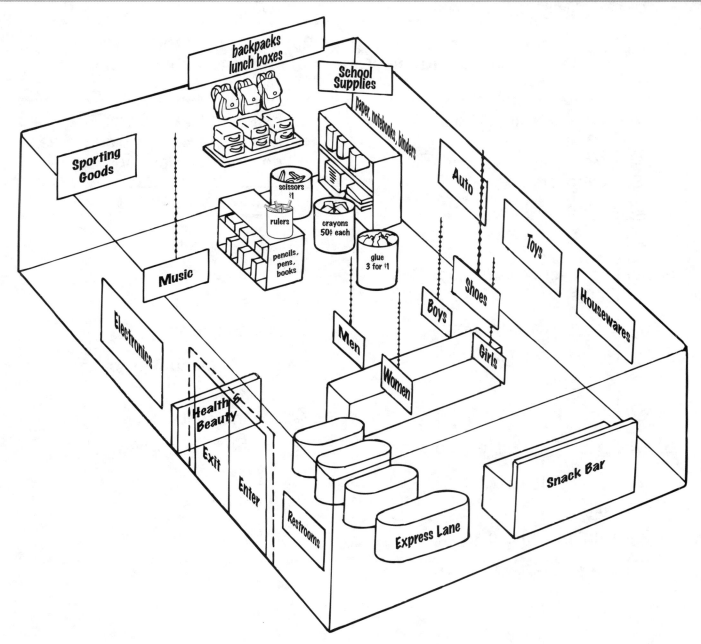

School starts in two weeks. Maria goes to the store. She gets school supplies. She has a list of what she needs.

Maria likes to shop for school. She looks at new crayons. She gets glitter pencils. She gets an eraser.

Maria chooses a backpack. She finds a lunch box she likes. She has almost everything she needs.

Back to School

Look at the picture on page 25. Read the story.
Use the picture and the story to answer the questions.

1. This story is mainly about

   (A) toys

   (B) school supplies

   (C) clothes

   (D) books

2. Maria got school *supplies*. She got things

   (A) she needs for school

   (B) she wants to play with

   (C) she needs to read

   (D) she wants to color

3. Where will Maria find an eraser?

   (A) with the paper

   (B) with the rulers

   (C) with the pencils

   (D) not at this store

4. Think about how the word *new* relates to *crayons*. Which words relate in the same way?

   | **new : crayons** |

   (A) shoes : exit

   (B) glue : scissors

   (C) ruler : binder

   (D) lunch : box

5. Where will Maria find school supplies?

   (A) by the snack bar

   (B) in the back corner

   (C) in electronics

   (D) by the toys

Going to the Movies

These are new words to practice.

Say each word 10 times.

* theater   * soon

* ticket   * attraction

* cinema   * llama

* entertainment   * matinee

Choose one new word to write.

_____

- -

_____

Going to the Movies

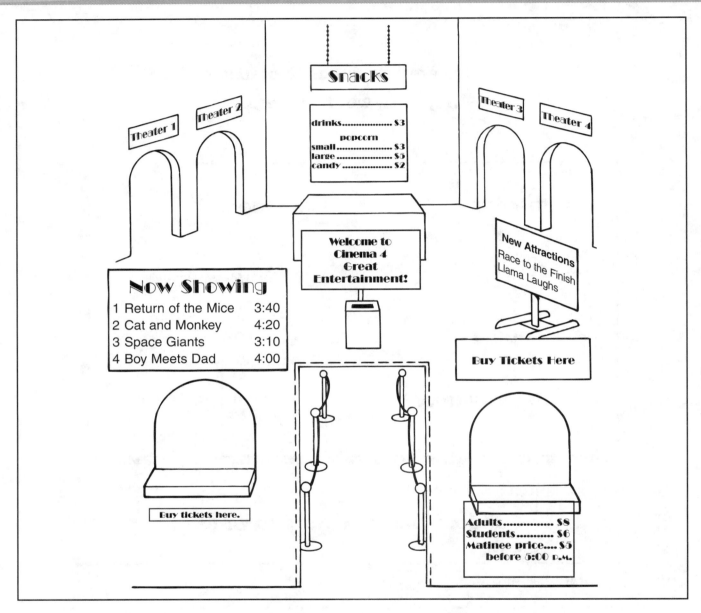

Snacks

drinks	$3
popcorn	
small	$3
large	$5
candy	$2

Welcome to Cinema 4 Great Entertainment!

New Attractions
Race to the Finish
Llama Laughs

Buy Tickets Here

Theater 1   Theater 2   Theater 3   Theater 4

Now Showing

1 Return of the Mice   3:40
2 Cat and Monkey   4:20
3 Space Giants   3:10
4 Boy Meets Dad   4:00

Buy tickets here.

Adults $8
Students $6
Matinee price $5
before 5:00 P.M.

Drew and his dad went to the movies. They got to the cinema at 3:20. They looked at the movie list.

They bought tickets. Each theater had a sign. It told which movie showed in that theater.

Drew found the right theater. He told his dad to go to Theater 1. They found seats.

Drew waited for the show to start. His dad said he could get a snack. He gave Drew some money. Drew went to the snack bar. He got popcorn and something to drink.

Drew went back to his seat. After he sat down, the show started. Drew and his dad enjoyed the movie.

Going to the Movies

**Look at the picture on page 28. Read the story.
Use the picture and the story to answer the questions.**

1. Drew went to the *cinema*. He can see

   (A) a game

   (B) a play

   (C) a movie

   (D) a concert

2. Drew may have popcorn and a drink. How much money will Drew need?

   (A) $5

   (B) $7

   (C) $3

   (D) $6

3. This story is mainly about

   (A) going to the movies

   (B) eating popcorn

   (C) running a race

   (D) catching mice

4. Drew got to the theater at 3:20. Which movie will he most likely see?

   (A) *Race to the Finish*

   (B) *Return of the Mice*

   (C) *Space Giants*

   (D) *Llama Laughs*

5. Think about how the word *cinema* relates to *theater*. Which words relate in the same way?

cinema : theater

   (A) now : soon

   (B) return : leave

   (C) dad : father

   (D) small : large

Hannah's Science Project

These are new words to practice.
Say each word 10 times.

* topic   * procedure

* project   * record

* hypothesis   * observe

* material   * conclusion

Choose one new word to write.

_____

- -

_____

Hannah's Science Project

Topic

My project is about plants.

Questions

Will a plant grow if I give it milk?

How much will a plant grow if it has milk?

Hypothesis

I think my plant will grow 2 inches.

Materials

plant

milk

Procedure

1. Measure plant.
2. Record the height.
3. Give plant $1/4$ cup milk.
4. Do steps 1–3 each day for 2 weeks.
5. Observe plant.
6. Record observations.
7. Form a conclusion.

Hannah did a science project at school. She chose a topic. She wrote questions and a hypothesis. She made a list of what she needed. She planned the steps she would need to do. Hannah wrote a procedure for her project. She did each step in order.

Hannah wanted her plant to grow. She gave it milk instead of water. She did this every day.

Each day Hannah measured the plant. She recorded the plant's height.

Hannah's plant grew one and a half inches. She thinks it likes milk.

Hannah's Science Project

**Read the sample project on page 31. Read the story.
Use the information and the story to answer the questions.**

1. How much milk did Hannah use?

   Ⓐ ¼ cup

   Ⓑ 3 ½ cups

   Ⓒ 5 drops

   Ⓓ 2 cups

2. This story is mainly about

   Ⓐ a plant

   Ⓑ a science procedure

   Ⓒ a ruler

   Ⓓ a cup of milk

3. Think about how the word *step* relates to *procedure*. Which words relate in the same way?

step : procedure

   Ⓐ plant : grow

   Ⓑ water : milk

   Ⓒ measure : materials

   Ⓓ item : list

4. Hannah made a list of *materials*. What was on her list?

   Ⓐ things for the project

   Ⓑ cloth

   Ⓒ healthful food

   Ⓓ nails and wood

5. Hannah will record the plant's height. First she must

   Ⓐ water the plant

   Ⓑ write her name

   Ⓒ watch the plant

   Ⓓ measure the plant

Helping Grandpa

These are new words to practice.
Say each word 10 times.

✳ chores	✳ leave
✳ garbage	✳ directions
✳ weed	✳ hand
✳ visited	✳ tool

Choose one new word to write.

Helping Grandpa

Philip,

I have to go to the store. Grandma is in the kitchen. Please do these chores.

1. Take out garbage
2. Pick up toys
3. Help Grandma with dishes
4. Weed flower bed

I will be back soon. Thank you for helping us!

Love,

Grandpa

Philip visited his grandparents. His grandpa gave him chores to do. Grandpa had to go to the store. He left directions for Philip.

Philip's grandma was working in the kitchen. She gave him some juice. She told him where to take the garbage.

Next he helped Grandma dry dishes. Grandma handed Philip the garden tools. She went out with him. They weeded the flowers together.

Helping Grandpa

**Read the letter on page 34. Read the story.
Use the letter and the story to answer the questions.**

1. What is this story mainly about?

   Ⓐ Grandma is washing dishes.

   Ⓑ Philip is visiting his grandparents.

   Ⓒ Philip is following directions.

   Ⓓ Grandpa is going to the store.

2. What did Grandma do after drying the dishes?

   Ⓐ She carried garden tools.

   Ⓑ She helped Philip garden.

   Ⓒ She showed Philip the clock.

   Ⓓ She gave Philip garden tools.

3. What did Philip do before he picked up his toys?

   Ⓐ He took out the garbage.

   Ⓑ He weeded the flowers.

   Ⓒ He washed the dishes.

   Ⓓ He read a book.

4. Why did Philip's grandpa ask him to do chores?

   Ⓐ Philip could get money.

   Ⓑ Philip would help Grandma.

   Ⓒ Philip would stay out of trouble.

   Ⓓ Philip would get a cookie.

5. Think about how the word *dry* relates to *dishes*. Which words relate in the same way?

dry : dishes

   Ⓐ grandma : grandpa

   Ⓑ store : kitchen

   Ⓒ throw : ball

   Ⓓ garden : tool

Listen Carefully

These are new words to practice.

Say each word 10 times.

* fold　　　　　　* flat

* half　　　　　　* closed

* lengthwise　　　* listen

* measure　　　　* exercise

Choose one new word to write.

_____

- - - - - - - - - - - - - - - - - - -

_____

Listen Carefully

☐ Measure 3 inches from the top of the paper. Draw a star.

☐ Draw a line on the fold line.

☐ On the left side of the paper, write three color words.

☐ Draw a 3-inch square on your paper. Color the square green.

☐ Fold your paper closed again.

☐ Put it in the basket at the front of the room.

Note to teacher: Read the right side of the page first.

You need a sheet of paper, a pencil, and a ruler. Fold your paper in half lengthwise. Open your paper flat. Write your name on the right half of the paper.

Brad's teacher read these directions aloud. The class followed the directions.

Brad was absent that day. Someone in his family will read the directions aloud. Then he will be able to do the listening exercise.

Brad's teacher copied the directions from the teacher's manual for Brad. Then he sent the paper home with Brad.

Brad's dad read the directions to him. Brad folded his paper. He wrote his name. He used his ruler and drew a circle.

Brad wrote three words. He drew a square and colored it green. Brad folded his paper. He put it in the basket.

Brad listened carefully. He followed most of the directions.

Listen Carefully

Read the directions on page 37. Read the story.
Use the directions and the story to answer the questions.

1. Brad's class did a listening *exercise*. They

   Ⓐ practiced a skill

   Ⓑ stayed healthy

   Ⓒ played an instrument

   Ⓓ did a math paper

2. This story is mainly about

   Ⓐ drawing a star

   Ⓑ folding a paper

   Ⓒ coloring a square

   Ⓓ listening to the teacher

3. Think about how the word *ruler* relates to *measure*. Which words relate in the same way?

   | ruler : measure |

   Ⓐ read : listen

   Ⓑ draw : color

   Ⓒ pencil : write

   Ⓓ fold : flat

4. Brad folded the paper. How did he fold it?

   Ⓐ widthwise

   Ⓑ lengthwise

   Ⓒ in fourths

   Ⓓ backward

5. Brad did not follow all of the directions. How can you tell?

   Ⓐ He drew a circle.

   Ⓑ He wrote his name.

   Ⓒ He folded his paper.

   Ⓓ He colored the square green.

Birthday Fun

These are new words to practice.
Say each word 10 times.

✳ party	✳ invitation
✳ towel	✳ forward
✳ sunglasses	✳ splash
✳ barbecue	✳ candle

Choose one new word to write.

_____

- -

_____

Birthday Fun

Please come!
Birthday Swim Party

When: *July 23*

3:00 P.M.

Where: *Merlin Lake*

Bring: *swimsuit, towel,*

sunglasses, sun lotion,

water toys

There will be a barbecue
after swimming.

Peter gave Hans an invitation. Peter is having a birthday party. Hans looks forward to the party.

The party will be at the lake. Hans and Peter will splash in the water. They might have a water fight. They will play tag in the sun.

Then Peter and Hans will eat. They will have barbecued hot dogs. They will have grapes.

Peter will open cards and presents. He will blow out candles on his birthday cake. Everyone will have a piece of cake. It will be a fun party.

Birthday Fun

**Look at the picture on page 40. Read the story.
Use the picture and the story to answer the questions.**

1. This story is mostly about

   Ⓐ the lake

   Ⓑ Peter's birthday party

   Ⓒ Peter's toys

   Ⓓ sunglasses

2. Hans will most likely

   Ⓐ go fishing

   Ⓑ go hiking

   Ⓒ go swimming

   Ⓓ go on a boat

3. Think about how the word *swim* relates to *lake*. Which words relate in the same way?

swim : lake

   Ⓐ ride : car

   Ⓑ come : stay

   Ⓒ swimsuit : towel

   Ⓓ birthday : party

4. At the *barbecue* Hans will eat

   Ⓐ a salad

   Ⓑ food from the kitchen

   Ⓒ food cooked outside

   Ⓓ crackers and cheese

5. Where is the party?

   Ⓐ at a barbecue

   Ⓑ in the grass

   Ⓒ at the pool

   Ⓓ at the lake

Junko Reads Directions

These are new words to practice.
Say each word 10 times.

✳ follow	✳ contraction
✳ careful	✳ apostrophe
✳ compound	✳ review
✳ connect	✳ example

Choose one new word to write.

_____

- - - - - - - - - - - - - - - - -

_____

Junko Reads Directions

Making New Words

Name: _____

Date: _____

Read the directions. Follow them carefully.

A. A compound word is made of two words. The two words make a new word. Look at the first example. Draw lines to connect words in each column. Write the new compound word.

1.	back	box	backpack _____
2.	drive	pack	_____
3.	news	land	_____
4.	mail	line	_____
5.	main	way	_____
6.	foot	door	_____
7.	side	paper	_____
8.	out	ball	_____

A. A contraction is two words put together. Use an apostrophe to show that letters have been left out. Write the two words that form each contraction.

1.	I'm	_____	_____
2.	can't	_____	_____
3.	couldn't	_____	_____
4.	she'll	_____	_____
5.	they're	_____	_____
6.	I've	_____	_____

Junko's class learned about words. Her teacher showed them compound words. He explained contractions.

The teacher gave the class this page. It helped them review these words.

Junko read the directions. She looked at the first example. It showed her how to do the work.

Junko drew lines to put words together. She wrote the compound words. She wrote the words from the contractions. Junko did not need any help.

Junko Reads Directions

**Read the directions on page 43. Read the story.
Use the directions and the story to answer the questions.**

1. A *contraction* is

   (A) something new

   (B) words crowded in a box

   (C) two words combined

   (D) a small word

2. Junko *followed* directions.

   (A) She walked behind the teacher.

   (B) She did what the directions said.

   (C) She asked for help.

   (D) She read a book.

3. This story is mainly about

   (A) going outdoors

   (B) drawing lines

   (C) writing words

   (D) reading directions

4. From the directions, you can tell

   (A) a mailbox has mail

   (B) two words will make one new word

   (C) an example does not help

   (D) a contraction has a comma

5. Think about how the word *follow* relates to *directions*. Which words relate in the same way?

   | follow : directions |

   (A) words : letters

   (B) explain : example

   (C) draw : write

   (D) walk : run

Wrapping a Gift

These are new words to practice.
Say each word 10 times.

✳ wrap	✳ loose
✳ nearly	✳ opposite
✳ enough	✳ desired
✳ cover	✳ instructions

Choose one new word to write.

_____

- - - - - - - - - - - - - - - -

_____

Wrapping a Gift

1. Place the box on the wrapping paper. Tape one edge of the paper to the side of the box.

2. Cut the paper so that it there is enough to cover the box. Tape the loose edge of the paper to the box.

3. Fold one end of the paper over the end of the box.

4. Fold in sides to form triangles.

5. Fold up the bottom end of the paper. Tape to the box.

6. Fold paper in the same way on the opposite end of the box.

7. Tape a bow or other decoration on top of the box if desired.

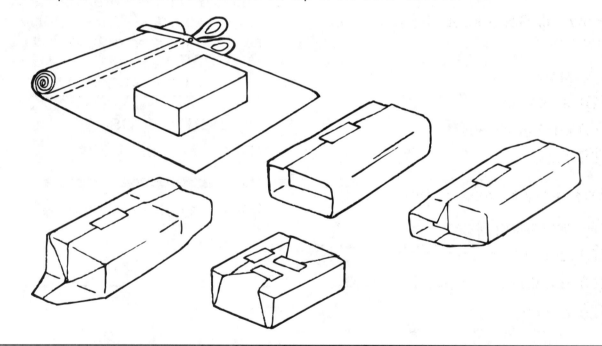

Dana's cousin invited her to a birthday party. Dana bought a gift and wrapping paper.

She also bought a bow that had a matching card. The package includes instructions that tell how to wrap a gift.

Dana read the instructions. She found a box nearly the same size as the gift. She put the gift in the box.

Dana followed the instructions. She wrapped the gift and taped a bow on top of the gift. Dana signed the card and taped it to the present.

Wrapping a Gift

Read the directions on page 46. Read the story.
Use the directions and the story to answer the questions.

1. Dana will use just enough paper to cover the gift. She will use

   Ⓐ the edges

   Ⓑ too much

   Ⓒ only what she needs

   Ⓓ a box

2. How will Dana keep the paper on the box?

   Ⓐ glue

   Ⓑ scissors

   Ⓒ rubber bands

   Ⓓ tape

3. This story is mostly about

   Ⓐ wrapping a gift

   Ⓑ going to a party

   Ⓒ helping someone

   Ⓓ cutting paper

4. Why did Dana wrap a box?

   Ⓐ to close it

   Ⓑ to give it as a gift

   Ⓒ to see what was inside

   Ⓓ to get help

5. Think about how the word *end* relates to *edge*. Which words relate in the same way?

end : edge

   Ⓐ tape : cut

   Ⓑ candle : party

   Ⓒ gift : present

   Ⓓ paper : bow

A Special Evening

These are new words to practice.
Say each word 10 times.

✳ VCR	✳ sound
✳ power	✳ remote control
✳ mute	✳ cartoons
✳ channel	✳ press

Choose one new word to write.

_____

- -

_____

48

A Special Evening

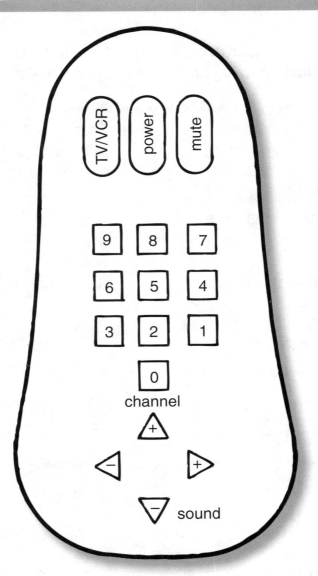

Jared's parents have gone out. They will be gone all evening. A neighbor will stay with him. Her name is Stacey.

Jared wants to watch cartoons. Stacey says okay. Jared may watch cartoons for one hour.

Jared gets the remote control. He pushes the power button. It turns on the TV.

He presses the four and then the two. Cartoons are on channel 42. It is time for "Walter's World."

Stacey asks Jared a question. She is standing in the kitchen. He presses the mute button. Now he can hear what she said.

Yes, Jared would like popcorn. Popcorn and cartoons are a special treat.

A Special Evening

**Look at the picture on page 49. Read the story.
Use the picture and the story to answer the questions.**

1. In this story, *mute* means

   Ⓐ to make quiet

   Ⓑ unable to speak

   Ⓒ something that plays music

   Ⓓ cannot hear

2. This story is mainly about

   Ⓐ eating popcorn

   Ⓑ seeing the neighbor

   Ⓒ using a remote control

   Ⓓ reading a book

3. Why did Jared use the remote control?

   Ⓐ to watch a DVD

   Ⓑ to listen to music

   Ⓒ to watch TV

   Ⓓ to play a video game

4. Think about how the word *hear* relates to *sound*. Which words relate in the same way?

hear : sound

   Ⓐ two : four

   Ⓑ mute : power

   Ⓒ channel : control

   Ⓓ ask : question

5. What did Jared want to watch?

   Ⓐ animals

   Ⓑ cartoons

   Ⓒ movies

   Ⓓ sports

Fun in the Garden

These are new words to practice.

Say each word 10 times.

* lettuce   * rake

* peas   * trowel

* corn   * vegetable

* hoe   * salad

Choose one new word to write.

_____

- -

_____

Fun in the Garden

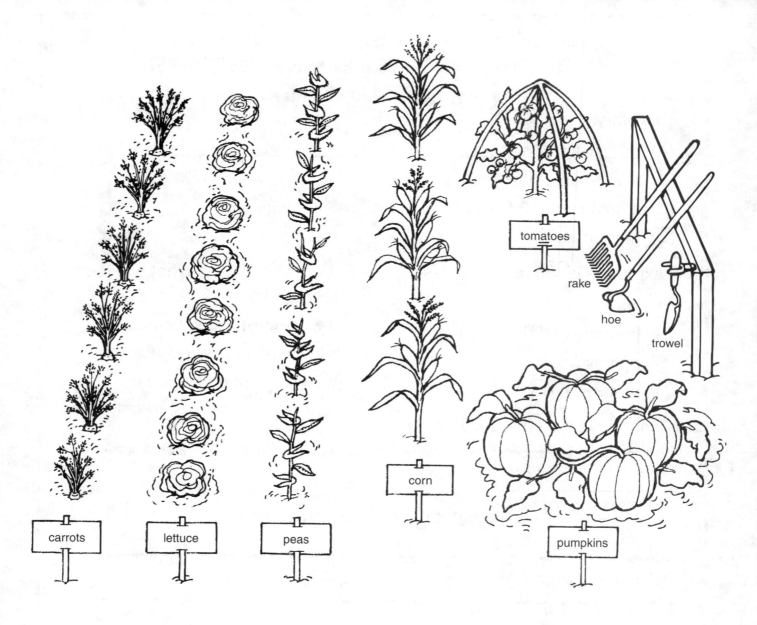

Lee helped her aunt plant a garden. They planted many vegetables. The garden is growing well.

Today Lee will help her aunt. They will weed the garden. Her aunt shows her the vegetable plants. Lee must pull out the weeds.

Her aunt hoes by the corn. Lee uses a trowel. She weeds the carrots.

The garden looks better now. Lee picks some vegetables. They will enjoy salad tonight.

Fun in the Garden

**Look at the picture on page 52. Read the story.
Use the picture and the story to answer the questions.**

1. This story is mainly about
   - (A) Lee's aunt
   - (B) a vegetable garden
   - (C) a salad
   - (D) garden tools

2. Next to the lettuce Lee planted
   - (A) corn
   - (B) tomatoes
   - (C) pumpkins
   - (D) peas

3. Think about how the word *carrot* relates to *vegetable*. Which words relate in the same way?

   | carrot : vegetable |

   - (A) plum : fruit
   - (B) large : garden
   - (C) weed : stick
   - (D) pick : pull

4. Lee's aunt used a *hoe* to
   - (A) make a hole
   - (B) get weeds out
   - (C) plant corn
   - (D) rake the grass

5. Lee likes salad. What would she most likely have in her salad?
   - (A) berries, nuts, lettuce
   - (B) pumpkin, lettuce, carrots
   - (C) corn, pumpkin, peas
   - (D) lettuce, carrots, tomato

After-School Snack

These are new words to practice.
Say each word 10 times.

✳ cranberry	✳ sift
✳ muffin	✳ batter
✳ liquid	✳ measure
✳ teaspoon	✳ ingredients

Choose one new word to write.

_____

- -

_____

After-School Snack

Cranberry Orange Muffins

Stir together:
1 egg
1/4 cup oil
1/2 cup milk
1/4 cup orange juice

Sift together and add to liquid:
1/2 cup sugar
1 1/2 cups flour
2 teaspoons baking powder
1/2 teaspoon salt

Stir in:
1/3 cup dried cranberries

Stir to mix all ingredients. Put muffin cups in muffin pan. Spoon batter into muffin cups. Bake at 400°F for 20 minutes.

Kian just got home from school. He wants to make a snack.

Kian's mom says he may make muffins. She will help with the oven. She helps Kian get things out.

Kian measures milk and oil. He cracks an egg. He adds orange juice. He stirs the liquid together.

Next Kian sifts the dry ingredients. He puts in the cranberries.

Mom gets the pan ready. She turns on the oven. Kian spoons batter into the pan. Mom puts the pan in the oven.

Kian looks forward to eating a warm muffin.

After-School Snack

Read the recipe on page 55. Read the story.
Use the recipe and the story to answer the questions.

1. *Liquid* is something you can

   Ⓐ pour

   Ⓑ chew

   Ⓒ play with

   Ⓓ melt

2. This story is mostly about

   Ⓐ picking oranges

   Ⓑ eating a snack

   Ⓒ making muffins

   Ⓓ cooking breakfast

3. How many eggs does Kian need?

   Ⓐ one

   Ⓑ two

   Ⓒ three

   Ⓓ none

4. What did Kian do before he added the orange juice?

   Ⓐ put in cranberries

   Ⓑ sift flour

   Ⓒ crack an egg

   Ⓓ turn on the oven

5. Think about how the word *milk* relates to *liquid.* Which words relate in the same way?

milk : liquid

   Ⓐ bake : oven

   Ⓑ cookie : solid

   Ⓒ measure : flour

   Ⓓ dry : water

David Knows How to Clean

These are new words to practice.

Say each word 10 times.

* bandage   * lip balm

* ointment   * medicine

* toothpaste   * first aid

* shampoo   * drawer

Choose one new word to write.

_____

- -

_____

David Knows How to Clean

David shares a bathroom with his sister, Liz. This week it is his turn to clean the bathroom.

David puts things away. He puts his comb in his drawer. He puts away the lip balm.

Liz cut her finger this morning. She has a bandage now. David puts away the bandages and the ointment.

He puts the shampoo back by the tub. He hangs up towels. He puts clean towels in the drawer.

David leaves the tissue and the soap on the counter. He uses cleanser to clean the sink. David wipes off the counter. The bathroom is clean now.

David Knows How to Clean

**Look at the picture on page 58. Read the story.
Use the picture and the story to answer the questions.**

1. This story is mainly about

    Ⓐ putting on a bandage

    Ⓑ taking a bath

    Ⓒ cleaning the bathroom

    Ⓓ wiping the counter

2. Where did David put the shampoo?

    Ⓐ in a drawer

    Ⓑ under the sink

    Ⓒ by the tub

    Ⓓ on the counter

3. In which drawer will David put the bandages?

    Ⓐ first aid

    Ⓑ towels

    Ⓒ David

    Ⓓ Liz

4. Liz put *ointment* on her cut. The ointment will

    Ⓐ make the bandage stick

    Ⓑ help it heal

    Ⓒ make it oily

    Ⓓ help it smell good

5. Think about how the word *bandages* relates to *first aid*. Which words relate in the same way?

    bandages : first aid

    Ⓐ ointment : lip balm

    Ⓑ shampoo : comb

    Ⓒ towel : hand

    Ⓓ tub : bathroom

A New House

These are new words to practice.
Say each word 10 times.

* beach   * festival

* seize   * unpack

* moment   * bare

* crab   * decoration

Choose one new word to write.

_____

- -

_____

60

A New House

Julie's family moved to a new house. They unpacked their things. The living room still looked bare.

Julie helped her mom. They hung up pictures. They put shells on a table. The shells are for decoration.

Julie's dad brought home a newspaper. He found another paper. It told about a crab festival. He got a tide table. It shows high tide and low tide. He put all the papers in the living room.

Julie's family likes their new house. The living room does not look bare any more!

A New House

**Look at the picture on page 61. Read the story.
Use the picture and the story to answer the questions.**

1. This story is mainly about

   Ⓐ Julie's toys

   Ⓑ Julie's friend

   Ⓒ Julie's new house

   Ⓓ Julie's picture

2. Where did Julie and her mom put the shells?

   Ⓐ on a table

   Ⓑ in a basket

   Ⓒ under the chair

   Ⓓ on the beach

3. The poster says "*Seize* the Moment." It means

   Ⓐ capture something and hide it

   Ⓑ take hold of this time to enjoy it

   Ⓒ grab the clock to make it stop

   Ⓓ take the poster off the wall

4. Think about how the word *shells* relate to *beach*. Which words relate in the same way?

   | shells : beach |

   Ⓐ crab : whale

   Ⓑ high : low

   Ⓒ walk : move

   Ⓓ whale : ocean

5. Julie's family most likely lives

   Ⓐ by a city

   Ⓑ by a lake

   Ⓒ by a forest

   Ⓓ by the ocean

Grandma's Kitchen

These are new words to practice.
Say each word 10 times.

* grandchild
* welcome
* grocery
* season

* calorie
* snack
* hang
* add

Choose one new word to write.

_____

- - - - - - - - - - - - - - - - - - -

_____

Grandma's Kitchen

After school Hayley goes to Grandma's house. She has a snack and visits with Grandma. Then she does her homework.

Hayley gives Grandma a card. It is Hayley's new soccer card. The card has Hayley's picture on it. Grandma hangs it on the refrigerator.

Today Hayley has to go to the doctor. She does not have much time.

Grandma sets out food for snack. Hayley can have fruit. She can have cheese and crackers.

The cheese is almost gone. Grandma adds cheese to the grocery list.

Hayley eats her snack. It is time to leave.

       64

Grandma's Kitchen

**Look at the picture on page 64. Read the story.
Use the picture and the story to answer the questions.**

1. Grandma has a *grocery* list. She needs to buy

   Ⓐ food
   Ⓑ garden tools
   Ⓒ clothes
   Ⓓ light bulbs

2. This story is mainly about

   Ⓐ Hayley's snack
   Ⓑ Grandma's kitchen
   Ⓒ Grandma's favorite food
   Ⓓ Bonnie's softball game

3. Think about how the word *grocery* relates to *list*. Which words relate in the same way?

   > **grocery : list**

   Ⓐ eggs : hen
   Ⓑ softball : soccer
   Ⓒ calorie : counter
   Ⓓ hot cocoa : candy

4. What items were already on Grandma's list?

   Ⓐ apples, milk, bread
   Ⓑ apples, eggs, cheese
   Ⓒ apples, milk, eggs
   Ⓓ apples, bread, eggs

5. Where is Hayley going today?

   Ⓐ to the store
   Ⓑ to the doctor
   Ⓒ to the softball game
   Ⓓ to the pizza place

Winter Vacation

These are new words to practice.
Say each word 10 times.

✳ news   ✳ Kwanzaa

✳ future   ✳ Hanukkah

✳ chef   ✳ preview

✳ custom   ✳ season

Choose one new word to write.

_____

- -

_____

Winter Vacation

Channel	Network	6:30	7:00	7:30	8:00	8:30	9:00
2	CBA	News	News	Future Finance	Ice Hockey		
6	BCS	News	Cool Man, Snow Man	Paws on Ice	Winter Hunt		Winter in Washington D.C.
8	NCB	Holiday Chef	Figure Skating		Christmas at Walter's		
10	SBP	Looking Ahead	Holiday Customs	Those Incredible Penguins		Holiday Music Magic	
12	SBC	News	Can You Believe It?	Real Holidays, Real People	Polar Bear Adventure		
22	KIDS	Chester Finds Christmas	Winter Tales	Kwanzaa Kids		Jael's Hanukkah Traditions	Surfin' Sam
49	BOX	News	Olympic Preview		Mitch's Mansion	Teen Daze	

This is the first day of winter vacation. Brett may watch TV. He does not have school tomorrow.

Brett decides to watch a holiday show. He looks at the TV guide. He will watch *Cool Man, Snow Man*.

The show is over now. Brett's family watches a movie. They watch *Polar Bear Adventure*.

Brett can see special shows. He likes the holiday season on TV.

Winter Vacation

**Read the schedule on page 67. Read the story.
Use the schedule and the story to answer the questions.**

1. Which show is most likely about a holiday?

   Ⓐ *Figure Skating*

   Ⓑ *Kwanzaa Kids*

   Ⓒ *Future Finance*

   Ⓓ *Mitch's Mansion*

2. After Brett watches a holiday show, he could still watch

   Ⓐ *News*

   Ⓑ *Holiday Chef*

   Ⓒ *Ice Hockey*

   Ⓓ *Chester Finds Christmas*

3. This story is mainly about

   Ⓐ watching TV

   Ⓑ going skating

   Ⓒ learning a game

   Ⓓ planning next year

4. Brett likes the holiday *season*. He likes

   Ⓐ summer

   Ⓑ salt and pepper

   Ⓒ this time of year

   Ⓓ this kind of music

5. Think about how the word *custom* relates to *tradition*. Which words relate in the same way?

   | custom : tradition |

   Ⓐ job : chore

   Ⓑ snow : rain

   Ⓒ Christmas : winter

   Ⓓ news : preview

Shooting Hoops

These are new words to practice.
Say each word 10 times.

* hoop ✻ tournament

* schedule ✻ half

* practice ✻ final

* coach ✻ champion

Choose one new word to write.

_____

- - - - - - - - - - - - - - - - - -

_____

Shooting Hoops

WESTFIELD TIMBERS
WINTER 2006-2007 SCHEDULE

⊕ **PRACTICE** ⊕

3:30–5:00 P.M.

Monday, Tuesday, Wednesday, Thursday

Westfield gym

⊕ **GAMES** ⊕

Saturday December 9—11:00 A.M. Reedville

Saturday December 16—1:00 P.M. Westfield

Saturday January 6—10:00 A.M. Baker Town

Sunday January 14—1:00 P.M. Westfield

Saturday January 20—10:00 A.M. Mountview

Sunday February 3—3:00 P.M. Baker Town*

You will get the schedule for the second half of the season.

⊕ **COACHES** ⊕

Josh Tate

Alan Sawyer

⊕ **TOURNAMENT** ⊕

Saturday–Sunday January 27–28

Reedville

Jessie plays basketball on a team. She got a schedule. It tells when the team practices. The schedule shows when they have games. It tells where the team plays. It shows the time for each game.

Jessie's team will play in a tournament. They will play more than one game. They will play many teams. One team will win the final game. They will be the champions.

70

Shooting Hoops

Read the schedule on page 70. Read the story.
Use the schedule and the story to answer the questions.

1. Jessie's team will play in a *tournament*. They will play

   (A) several games in a contest

   (B) on horses

   (C) a game of chess

   (D) one game away from home

2. This story is mainly about

   (A) a girl

   (B) a basketball schedule

   (C) a coach

   (D) a football game

3. Which statement is not true?

   (A) The schedule tells practice times.

   (B) The schedule tells game times.

   (C) The schedule tells about a team party.

   (D) The schedule tells the coaches' names.

4. What is Jessie's team called?

   (A) Westfield Timbers

   (B) Reedville Rockets

   (C) Mountview Eagles

   (D) Baker Town Bobcats

5. Think about how the word *coach* relates to *team*. Which words relate in the same way?

coach : team

   (A) game : tournament

   (B) move : play

   (C) final : last

   (D) mayor : city

Scout Events

These are new words to practice.
Say each word 10 times.

* event   * meet

* pack   * trail

* calendar   * carpool

* regular   * fund

Choose one new word to write.

_____

- -

_____

Scout Events

Pack 556

Summer Calendar

Day	Date	Time	Activity	Place	Please Bring
Mondays		7:00 P.M.	Regular Meeting	Crestline School	
Saturday	May 19	10:00 A.M.	Bike Ride	Freedom Trail	water and sack lunch
Friday–Sunday	June 15–17	4:00 P.M.	Campout	Crestline School (We will carpool to Camp Colville)	camping gear.
Saturday	June 30	10:00 A.M.	Car Wash Fund Raiser	Crestline School	
Wednesday	July 4	3:00 P.M.	Family Picnic & Fireworks	Davis Park	food and lawn chairs
Saturday	July 21	10:00 P.M.	Kayak Trip	Round Lake	sack lunch
Sunday	August 12–18	2:00 P.M.	Scout Camp	Crestline School	

Kevin belongs to a Cub Scout pack. They like to do things together. They have activities planned for the summer.

Kevin went to a Scout meeting. The leader gave him this schedule. It shows the pack's summer activities.

Kevin likes to camp. He will go on the camping trip. He doesn't like to swim. He may not go on the kayak trip.

It looks like a fun summer. Kevin is glad he is a Cub Scout.

Scout Events

**Look at the chart on page 73. Read the story.
Use the chart and the story to answer the questions.**

1. This story is mainly about

   (A) a picnic and fireworks
   (B) scout camp
   (C) summer scout events
   (D) regular scout meetings

2. When is the bike ride?

   (A) June 17
   (B) August 18
   (C) July 21
   (D) May 19

3. The pack will have a fundraiser. They will

   (A) give money to other scouts
   (B) get money for camp
   (C) lift supplies into a truck
   (D) wash cars for fun

4. Think about how the word *lunch* relates to *picnic*. Which words relate in the same way?

   lunch : picnic

   (A) food : water
   (B) tent : campout
   (C) calendar : event
   (D) sack : bag

5. What will Kevin most likely take when he goes camping?

   (A) a tent
   (B) a bunk bed
   (C) a hammock
   (D) a computer

Lessons for Luke

These are new words to practice.
Say each word 10 times.

✳ lesson	✳ after
✳ piano	✳ practice
✳ tutor	✳ each
✳ notes	✳ fee

Choose one new word to write.

_____

- - - - - - - - - - - - - - - - - - - -

_____

Lessons for Luke

NOTES	DAY	DATE	TIME
Please practice piano 20–30 minutes each day. lessons $12 per week piano books $20 math fees $10	Tuesday	June 26	tutor 2:00 P.M. piano 3:00 P.M.
	Thursday	June 28	tutor 10:00 A.M.
	Tuesday	July 3	tutor 2:00 P.M. piano 3:00 P.M.
	Tuesday	July 10	tutor 2:00 P.M. piano 3:00 P.M.
	Thursday	July 12	tutor 10:00 A.M.
	Tuesday	July 17	teacher out of town
	Thursday	July 19	teacher out of town
	Tuesday	July 24	tutor 2:00 P.M. piano 3:00 P.M.
	Thursday	July 26	tutor 10:00 A.M.
	Tuesday	July 31	tutor 2:00 P.M. piano 3:00 P.M.
	Thursday	August 2	tutor 10:00 A.M.
	Tuesday	August 7	Luke at camp
	Thursday	August 9	Luke at camp
	Tuesday	August 14	tutor 2:00 P.M. piano 3:00 P.M.
	Thursday	August 16	tutor 10:00 A.M.

This summer Luke will have lessons. He will take piano lessons. He will have a tutor.

Luke will have piano lessons on Tuesdays. His friend Charles will also take piano lessons.

Luke will meet with the tutor two days a week. Luke will work on math. He will practice writing.

Luke will not see the tutor after school starts. He will still take piano lessons in the winter.

Lessons for Luke

**Look at the schedule on page 76. Read the story.
Use the schedule and the story to answer the questions.**

1. How often should Luke practice piano?

   (A) once a week

   (B) every day

   (C) when he wants to

   (D) two days a week

2. This story is mostly about

   (A) Luke's lessons

   (B) Luke's friend

   (C) Luke's camp

   (D) Luke's tutor

3. Think about how the word *summer* relates to *winter*. Which words relate in the same way?

   | **summer : winter** |

   (A) math : writing

   (B) practice : piano

   (C) begin : end

   (D) tutor : lesson

4. On Tuesdays, Luke will

   (A) go to the pool

   (B) hear a concert

   (C) play soccer

   (D) see Charles

5. Luke will have a *tutor*. A tutor is someone

   (A) who teaches large groups

   (B) who plays a flute

   (C) who teaches one student at a time

   (D) who teaches friends

Water World

These are new words to practice.
Say each word 10 times.

* shuttle   * terminal

* arrive   * theme

* depart   * hotel

* catch   * free

Choose one new word to write.

_____

- - - - - - - - - - - - - - - - - - - -

_____

Water World

Free Shuttle Bus

Water World		Hotels	
Depart	**Arrive**	**Depart**	**Arrive**
10:30	10:20	10:00	10:50
11:30	11:20	11:00	11:50
1:00	12:50	12:30	1:20
2:00	1:50	1:30	2:20
3:00	2:50	2:30	3:20
4:00	3:50	3:30	4:20
5:00	4:50	4:30	5:20
6:00	5:50	5:30	6:20
7:00	6:50	6:30	7:20
8:00	7:50	7:30	8:20
9:00	8:50	8:30	9:20

Shuttle runs 10:00 A.M.–9:00 P.M.
Hotels to Water World
Shuttle departs every hour
Water World to Hotels
Shuttle departs every hour
* Catch the shuttle at blue terminal A

Darcy's family took a vacation. They went to Water World. It is a theme park.

They stayed at a hotel. The hotel was not next to Water World.

Darcy's family could ride a shuttle bus. It would take them to Water World. The bus was free.

They took the shuttle bus to Water World. They played on water slides.

Darcy was hungry. She wanted to go to the hotel. She wanted to eat lunch.

It was 11:15. Darcy waited for the next bus. She had to wait 15 minutes.

After lunch they caught the bus. They went back to Water World. The bus helped Darcy's family.

Water World

Read the schedule on page 79. Read the story.
Use the schedule and the story to answer the questions.

1. Darcy will *catch* a shuttle bus. She will

   Ⓐ get on the bus
   Ⓑ get off the bus
   Ⓒ stop the bus
   Ⓓ watch for the bus

2. How long did Darcy have to wait?

   Ⓐ 30 minutes
   Ⓑ 15 minutes
   Ⓒ 20 minutes
   Ⓓ 10 minutes

3. This story is mainly about

   Ⓐ taking a vacation
   Ⓑ going to the water
   Ⓒ eating lunch
   Ⓓ riding a shuttle bus

4. The shuttle bus goes from the

   Ⓐ hotel to the airport
   Ⓑ terminal to Water World
   Ⓒ hotel to Water World
   Ⓓ terminal to Darcy's house

5. Think about how the word *go* relates to *stay*. Which words relate in the same way?

   go : stay

   Ⓐ hungry : eat
   Ⓑ arrive : depart
   Ⓒ shuttle : bus
   Ⓓ hotel : park

80

Classroom Jobs

These are new words to practice.

Say each word 10 times.

* salute   * tomorrow

* leader   * job

* count   * chart

* floor   * remind

Choose one new word to write.

_____

- -

_____

Classroom Jobs

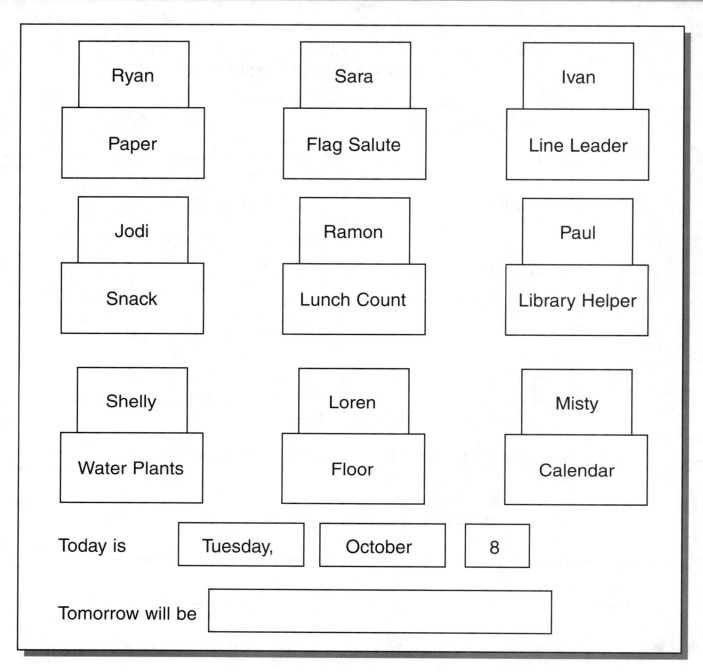

| Ryan | Sara | Ivan |
| Paper | Flag Salute | Line Leader |

| Jodi | Ramon | Paul |
| Snack | Lunch Count | Library Helper |

| Shelly | Loren | Misty |
| Water Plants | Floor | Calendar |

Today is | Tuesday, | October | 8

Tomorrow will be

Ramon's class has a job chart. Children take turns doing jobs. Each job helps the class.

Today Ramon is the lunch count person. He will count how many people have cold lunch. He will count the people who want hot lunch. He will count the people who will just buy milk.

Tomorrow Ramon's job will be library helper. He will remind people to put books away. He will help keep the classroom library neat. This is Ramon's favorite job.

Classroom Jobs

**Look at the picture on page 82. Read the story.
Use the picture and the story to answer the questions.**

1. Who has the job of watering the plants?

    (A) Jodi

    (B) Paul

    (C) Shelly

    (D) Loren

2. What day of the week will it be tomorrow?

    (A) Monday

    (B) Wednesday

    (C) Thursday

    (D) Friday

3. This story is mainly about

    (A) classroom rules

    (B) classroom pets

    (C) classroom books

    (D) classroom jobs

4. The line *leader*

    (A) takes charge of the class

    (B) walks at the front of the line

    (C) tells people how to walk in line

    (D) wears a leash

5. Think about how the word *hot* relates to *cold*. Which words relate in the same way?

hot : cold

    (A) snack : lunch

    (B) today : tomorrow

    (C) job : help

    (D) leader : follower

Walking on the Beach

These are new words to practice.
Say each word 10 times.

✳ beach   ✳ print

✳ tide   ✳ exposed

✳ light   ✳ sand

✳ bold   ✳ rock

Choose one new word to write.

_____

- -

_____

Walking on the Beach

July Tide Table

High Tide   Low Tide

Date	Time	Feet	Time	Feet	Date	Time	Feet	Time	Feet
1	3:30	6.5	**6:00**	**5.5**	1	11:00	0	**11:15**	**3**
2	4:30	5	**6:45**	**6**	2	11:45	0		
3	5:30	5	**7:30**	**6**	3	12:30	3	**12:30**	**0**
4	6:45	5	**8:00**	**6**	4	1:30	2.5	**1:15**	**1**
5	8:00	4.5	**8:45**	**6.5**	5	2:45	2	**2:00**	**1.5**
6	9:15	4.5	**9:15**	**7**	6	3:30	1.5	**2:45**	**2**
7	10:30	4.5	**9:45**	**7**	7	4:15	0.5	**3:30**	**2.5**
8	11:30	5	**10:15**	**7.5**	8	5:00	0	**4:15**	**3**
9	**12:15**	5	**11:00**	**7.5**	9	5:45	-0.5	**5:00**	**3**
10	**1:00**	5.5	**11:30**	**8**	10	6:15	-1	**5:45**	**3**

A.M. light print   P.M. **bold print**

Fonda and her family will go to the beach July 6–9. At low tide, the water is farther out. There is more sand exposed on the beach. Fonda can look for shells.

During high tide, the water covers most of the beach. Fonda has to walk between rocks and watch carefully for high waves.

Fonda looks at the tide table. The best time to walk on the beach is early morning. Then the tide is lowest.

Walking on the Beach

**Look at the chart on page 85. Read the story.
Use the chart and the story to answer the questions.**

1. This story is mainly about

   Ⓐ morning and evening

   Ⓑ high tide and low tide

   Ⓒ hands and feet

   Ⓓ sand and rocks

2. Which day has only one low tide?

   Ⓐ July 2

   Ⓑ July 1

   Ⓒ July 3

   Ⓓ July 9

3. When is the best time for Fonda to walk on the beach?

   Ⓐ night

   Ⓑ high tide

   Ⓒ low tide

   Ⓓ during a storm

4. Think about how the word *light* relates to *bold*. Which words relate in the same way?

light : bold

   Ⓐ low : high

   Ⓑ tide : water

   Ⓒ time : date

   Ⓓ beach : shells

5. The change in sea level is called the

   Ⓐ wave

   Ⓑ flow

   Ⓒ tide

   Ⓓ swell

Reading a Textbook

These are new words to practice.
Say each word 10 times.

* energy   * study

* health   * textbook

* diet   * heading

* fat   * bold

Choose one new word to write.

_____

- -

_____

Reading a Textbook

EATING FOR HEALTH

Your body gets energy from food. Food helps your body grow. You need good food to stay healthy.

There are four main food groups: dairy, meat, grain, and fruits and vegetables. Each day you should eat food from each group.

A healthful **diet** has lots of fruits and vegetables. It has food from the other food groups. It does not have much **sugar** or **fat**.

Review what you just read.

1. Write the four food groups.

   _____   _____

   _____   _____

2. Write one example of each type of food.

   _____   _____

   _____   _____

3. Which things should you not eat too much of?

   _____   _____

   _____   _____

Erica's class will study something new. Their teacher gives each person a textbook. It is a health book.

Mr. Morse tells the class that this section has a heading. The heading has capital letters.

He also says some words are in bold print. Erica should learn the words in bold. They will help her understand what she reads.

Erica will read this page. She will do the review questions. She will write her answers on a sheet of paper.

88

Reading a Textbook

**Read the sample textbook page on page 88. Read the story.
Use the textbook page and the story to answer the questions.**

1. The *heading* is

   Ⓐ a title for that page

   Ⓑ a hat you wear

   Ⓒ a way to hit a ball

   Ⓓ a place to write your name

2. This story is mainly about

   Ⓐ growing taller

   Ⓑ writing answers

   Ⓒ reading a page in a textbook

   Ⓓ learning new words

3. Think about how the word *write* relates to *answer*. Which words relate in the same way?

   write : answer

   Ⓐ food : energy

   Ⓑ color : picture

   Ⓒ grow : healthy

   Ⓓ diet : eat

4. What kind of textbook did Erica read?

   Ⓐ a math book

   Ⓑ a history book

   Ⓒ a science book

   Ⓓ a health book

5. Which statement is not true?

   Ⓐ Erica will answer questions.

   Ⓑ Erica will learn new words.

   Ⓒ Erica will eat in class.

   Ⓓ Erica will read the page.

Meet a Geographer

These are new words to practice.
Say each word 10 times.

* resource   * college

* climate   * biography

* people   * essay

* landform   * remember

Choose one new word to write.

_____

- -

_____

Meet a Geographer

Edward Webb

1927–2000

A geographer studies geography. He learns about the world's natural resources.

He studies the climate. He looks at landforms. He studies people too.

Edward Webb traveled to many places. He took pictures. He wrote notes. He came back and taught his students.

Mr. Webb wrote a textbook. It is a geography book.

College students read the book. They learn more about our world.

Mr. Webb spoke at schools. He told students about the places he had been.

Many people learned from Mr. Webb. They wanted to learn about geography, too.

Ted reads a biography. He reads about someone else's life.

This short essay tells about Edward Webb. It tells when he lived. It tells what he did. The biography tells why people remember him.

Ted learns about Mr. Webb. He wishes he could meet Mr. Webb. He would like to see the pictures.

Mr. Webb has died. Ted cannot meet him.

Meet a Geographer

**Read the biography on page 91. Read the story.
Use the biography and the story to answer the questions.**

1. This story is mainly about

   (A) a picture

   (B) a geographer

   (C) a globe

   (D) a college student

2. What did Mr. Webb write?

   (A) a textbook

   (B) a letter

   (C) a story

   (D) a poem

3. Why do people remember Edward Webb?

   (A) he wrote notes

   (B) he liked to travel

   (C) he took many pictures

   (D) many people learned from him

4. Think about how the word *short* relates to *essay*. Which words relate in the same way?

short : essay

   (A) lived : died

   (B) geography : climate

   (C) write : speak

   (D) beautiful : picture

5. Ted read a *biography*. It is about

   (A) pictures

   (B) a person's life

   (C) an animal

   (D) school

Come to the Science Fair

These are new words to practice.

Say each word 10 times.

* model   * quality

* shuttle   * demonstration

* enter   * display

* project   * participate

Choose one new word to write.

_____

- - - - - - - - - - - - - - - - - -

_____

Come to the Science Fair

Sunset School Science Fair
Thursday, March 22
6:30–8:30 P.M.

Enter your project in the fair.

★

Get an entry form from your teacher.

See a model of the space shuttle Challenger.

See science demonstrations and displays.

Prizes will be awarded for creative, quality work.

Participate in fun activities.

* Mrs. Gilbert's class—get 10 extra class points if you come to the fair!

Mrs. Gilbert gave each student this flier. It tells about the science fair. The fair will be at the school.

Mandy started working on a project. She gathered wildflowers from the mountains. Now she will write the names of the flowers.

Mandy wants to enter the fair. She gets an entry form from her teacher. Mandy works carefully. She hopes her project will win.

Come to the Science Fair

**Look at the picture on page 94. Read the story.
Use the picture and the story to answer the questions.**

1. What can Mandy do at the fair?

   (A) draw a picture

   (B) ride in a space shuttle

   (C) see a display

   (D) work on a project

2. Mandy can see a science *demonstration*. She can see

   (A) how to win a prize

   (B) how to read a book

   (C) how people get upset

   (D) how to do a science experiment

3. This story is mainly about

   (A) a science fair

   (B) a science teacher

   (C) a space shuttle

   (D) a science activity

4. What will Mandy get if she goes to the science fair?

   (A) a prize

   (B) extra class points

   (C) a space shuttle model

   (D) an entry form

5. Think about how the word *enter* relates to *fair*. Which words relate in the same way?

   > **enter : fair**

   (A) win : prize

   (B) space : shuttle

   (C) class : student

   (D) model : display

Today's News for Today's Kids

These are new words to practice.
Say each word 10 times.

✳ news	✳ interview
✳ usually	✳ conserve
✳ provide	✳ magazine
✳ question	✳ article

Choose one new word to write.

_____

- -

_____

Today's News for Today's Kids

IN THE NEWS

In the fall, it usually rains in the northwest. This year, the sun is shining. It has only rained four days.

This is good news for Christmas tree farmers. It is easy to cut and ship the trees. Many Christmas trees come from Oregon and Washington.

When it doesn't rain, no snow falls in the mountains. Winter snow provides water in the summer. The snow melts and runs into rivers and lakes. Next summer there might not be enough water for the crops.

Interview

Miss Vicky

Reading Room has a new reader! Miss Vicky will read stories every Tuesday. Watch on KIDS at 8:30 A.M.

Top 5 Sports

soccer | football | baseball | swimming | running

1,000 third graders

Thought Question

How can you conserve water ?

Every week Dawn gets a news magazine. She reads the articles. Then her class talks about the magazine.

This week Dawn reads a story about weather. She learns that farmers need water for crops. In the summer, they can get water when the snow melts.

Dawn sees a graph. It tells what sports children like best. She thinks this week's magazine has good things to know.

Today's News for Today's Kids

**Look at the sample magazine page on page 97. Read the story.
Use the magazine page and the story to answer the questions.**

1. When can Dawn watch *Reading Room*?

   Ⓐ today

   Ⓑ in the fall

   Ⓒ Tuesday morning

   Ⓓ next year

2. This magazine tells about things that just happened. It tells the

   Ⓐ teacher

   Ⓑ news

   Ⓒ story

   Ⓓ weather

3. This story is mainly about

   Ⓐ a news magazine

   Ⓑ a farmer

   Ⓒ a sport

   Ⓓ a mountain

4. Think about how the word *crops* relates to *water*. Which words relate in the same way?

crops : water

   Ⓐ news : next

   Ⓑ news : magazine

   Ⓒ children : food

   Ⓓ reading : sports

5. The news story tells about the weather in

   Ⓐ the south

   Ⓑ the Reading Room

   Ⓒ the United States

   Ⓓ the northwest

Wonderful Wildcats

These are new words to practice.
Say each word 10 times.

* species
* include

* picture
* nonfiction

* caption
* fact

* which
* text

Choose one new word to write.

_____

- - - - - - - - - - - - - - - - - - -

_____

Wonderful Wildcats

This cat has patches.
Jaguars live in Mexico and
South America.

Tigers are the largest
of the cats. They live in
Asia.

Leopards have spotted coats.
They may be found in Africa.

This cat runs quickly. It lives
in Africa and southern Asia.

The cat family has many species. Look at the pictures. Read the captions.
Where do big cats live? Which cat is the largest?
Smaller wildcats include the bobcat and the lynx. How do you think these wildcats would be
different from your pet cat?

Diego checks out a library book. It is a book about wildcats. Diego likes to read about animals.

This book is nonfiction. It is not a story. It has true facts. It has pictures and captions.

Diego wants to know more about the pictures. He can read the captions.

The text asks questions. Diego reads the questions. They help him think about what he reads.

Diego thinks about the answers to the questions. He will remember what he reads. He can
tell his friends and family about wildcats.

Wonderful Wildcats

**Look at the picture on page 100. Read the story.
Use the sample page and the story to answer the questions.**

1. This story is mainly about

   Ⓐ having a pet cat

   Ⓑ reading a nonfiction book

   Ⓒ answering a question

   Ⓓ reading a story

2. Where do several wildcats live?

   Ⓐ Africa

   Ⓑ North America

   Ⓒ Australia

   Ⓓ Europe

3. Why does Diego read the *captions*?

   Ⓐ to catch a wildcat

   Ⓑ to take a picture

   Ⓒ to find out about the pictures

   Ⓓ to get a library book

4. Think about how the word *large* relates to *small*. Which words relate in the same way?

   large : small

   Ⓐ tiger : leopard

   Ⓑ Africa : Asia

   Ⓒ pictures : text

   Ⓓ wild : tame

5. The cat family has many species. *Species* means

   Ⓐ spots

   Ⓑ groups

   Ⓒ diseases

   Ⓓ homes

Learning About the Dictionary

These are new words to practice.
Say each word 10 times.

✳ noun	✳ guide
✳ verb	✳ alphabetical
✳ adjective	✳ meaning
✳ dictionary	✳ definition

Choose one new word to write.

_____

- -

_____

Learning About the Dictionary

---

final   **fun**

final (fin-al) *adjective* the very last

fins (finz)
      1. *noun* part of a fish   *The fish has small fins.*
      2. *noun* large pieces of rubber people can wear to help them swim

fish (fish)
      1. *noun* an animal that lives in water and swims
      2. *verb* to catch such an animal, usually with a pole and bait

freeze (frez) verb to keep cold enough that water will turn to ice

fun (fun)
      1. *adjective* enjoyable
      2. *noun* to have fun; to do something for pleasure

Lynn's teacher shows the class this dictionary page. The teacher tells how to use the dictionary.

There are bold words at the top. They are guide words. Guide words tell the first and last words on a page. The words are listed in alphabetical order.

A dictionary tells how to use a word. It tells if a word is a noun. It tells if it is a verb or adjective. It might give a sample sentence.

Some words have more than one meaning. Often the most common definition is listed first.

Lynn learns to use the dictionary. The class dictionary has pictures. It is fun to read.

Learning About the Dictionary

**Look at the sample dictionary page on page 103. Read the story.
Use the sample page and the story to answer the questions.**

1. A *dictionary* tells

   Ⓐ which way to go

   Ⓑ how to write sentences

   Ⓒ what words mean

   Ⓓ where to find information

2. This story is mainly about

   Ⓐ the alphabet

   Ⓑ the ocean

   Ⓒ the freezer

   Ⓓ the dictionary

3. Think about how the word *fish* relates to *noun*. Which words relate in the same way?

fish : noun

   Ⓐ first : last

   Ⓑ run : verb

   Ⓒ word : sentence

   Ⓓ fresh : frozen

4. How does the dictionary list words?

   Ⓐ by nouns, verbs, or adjectives

   Ⓑ in alphabetical order

   Ⓒ by definition

   Ⓓ in number order

5. Which word could Lynn find on this page?

   Ⓐ friend

   Ⓑ family

   Ⓒ funny

   Ⓓ fill

Camping at the Beach

These are new words to practice.
Say each word 10 times.

* restroom   * vehicle

* electrical   * ranger

* site   * maximum

* host   * limit

Choose one new word to write.

_____

- -

_____

Camping at the Beach

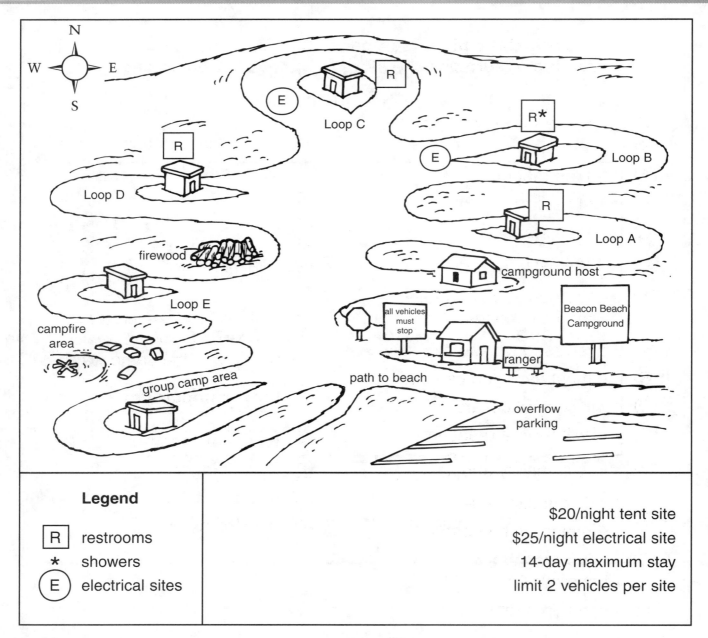

Legend

R restrooms
* showers
E electrical sites

$20/night tent site
$25/night electrical site
14-day maximum stay
limit 2 vehicles per site

Jennifer's family went camping. They went to the beach. They will sleep in a tent.

They drove into the campground. First they had to stop at the ranger station. The ranger gave them a camp site number. They will stay on loop D. He gave them a map of the campground.

Jennifer used the map. She showed her dad on the map where to get firewood. She walked with him and helped him get the wood.

Later Jennifer walked around the campground. She said hello to the campground host. She saw the campfire area. She found the path to the beach.

Camping at the Beach

**Look at the picture on page 106. Read the story.
Use the picture and the story to answer the questions.**

1. Where did Jennifer's family get the map?

   Ⓐ from the ranger

   Ⓑ in the mail

   Ⓒ from the store

   Ⓓ at the beach

2. The campground has a 14-day *maximum*. That means

   Ⓐ the fewest days you can stay

   Ⓑ the most days you can stay

   Ⓒ it will cost 14 dollars

   Ⓓ you will have a great time

3. This story is mainly about

   Ⓐ building a campfire

   Ⓑ swimming at the beach

   Ⓒ getting around the campground

   Ⓓ setting up a tent

4. Jennifer found the path to the beach. Which direction did she walk?

   Ⓐ west

   Ⓑ east

   Ⓒ north

   Ⓓ south

5. Think about how the word *tent* relates to *campground*. Which words relate in the same way?

   tent : campground

   Ⓐ restroom : shower

   Ⓑ host : ranger

   Ⓒ wood : fire

   Ⓓ day : night

What's the Weather?

These are new words to practice.
Say each word 10 times.

✳ weather	✳ forecast
✳ partly	✳ wind
✳ sunny	✳ blow
✳ cloudy	✳ chance

Choose one new word to write.

_____

- - - - - - - - - - - - - - - - -

_____

What's the Weather?

partly sunny
66°F
10 NW
Monday

cloudy
rain 50%
63°F
15 SW
Tuesday

cloudy
rain 60%
61°F
10 SW
Wednesday

partly
cloudy
65°F
10 SE
Thursday

sunny
68°F
calm
Friday

Key

 cloud

sun

★ snow

 rain

Catherine wants to know what the weather will be like this week. She asks her dad what he thinks. He shows her the weather forecast on TV.

Catherine's family lives in the northeast. Her dad explains the wind will blow from the southwest. That often means it will rain. He says there is a chance of rain on Tuesday and Wednesday.

Catherine wants to ride bikes with her friends. She thinks Friday will be the best day for bike riding. She is glad it won't rain all week.

What's the Weather?

Look at the picture on page 109. Read the story.
Use the picture and the story to answer the questions.

1. This story is mainly about
   - (A) the rain yesterday
   - (B) the wind on Saturday
   - (C) the snow in the mountains
   - (D) the weather this week

2. The TV showed a *weather forecast*. It told
   - (A) what weather happened yesterday
   - (B) what kind of hat the weather man has
   - (C) what the weather man believes will happen
   - (D) what everyone wants to happen

3. What will the weather be on Wednesday?
   - (A) sunny with wind
   - (B) cloudy with rain
   - (C) foggy with rain
   - (D) snowy with wind

4. Think about how the word *rain* relates to *sun*. Which words relate in the same way?

   rain : sun

   - (A) chance : might
   - (B) wind : calm
   - (C) weather : forecast
   - (D) northwest : north

5. From which direction will the wind blow on Thursday?
   - (A) southeast
   - (B) northeast
   - (C) southwest
   - (D) northwest

Making a Map

These are new words to practice.
Say each word 10 times.

* community   * bridge

* map   * label

* compass rose   * road

* legend   * symbol

Choose one new word to write.

_____

- -

_____

Making a Map

Our Community

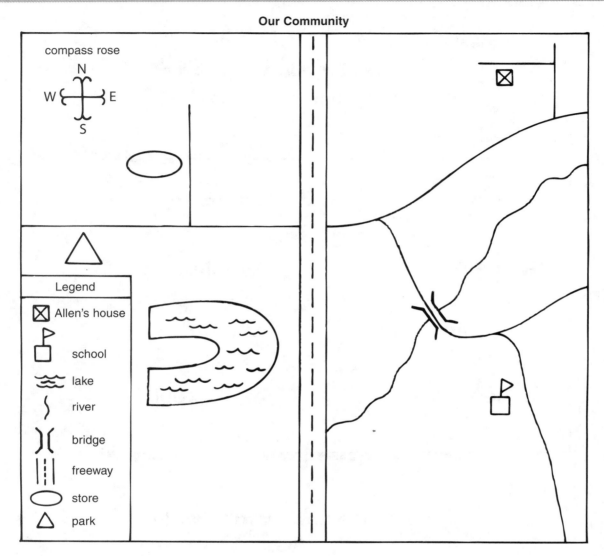

Allen's class learned about maps. They practiced making maps. Each person drew a map of their community.

Mrs. Baker helped the class get started. She drew a sample on the board. She drew the river and the freeway. Mrs. Baker wrote labels. She showed the class how to draw a compass rose.

Allen added roads to his map. He drew the school on his map. He put his house on the map. He added other places, too.

Allen put a legend on his map. He showed the symbols he used. He told the meaning of the symbols.

Allen colored the map. His map is easy to read.

Making a Map

Look at the picture on page 112. Read the story.
Use the picture and the story to answer the questions.

1. Allen colored his map. What color did he most likely use for the lake?

   Ⓐ brown
   Ⓑ green
   Ⓒ blue
   Ⓓ yellow

2. This story is mainly about

   Ⓐ going to school
   Ⓑ drawing a map
   Ⓒ coloring a picture
   Ⓓ planting a rose

3. Think about how the word *river* relates to *bridge*. Which words relate in the same way?

river : bridge

   Ⓐ mountain : tunnel
   Ⓑ legend : symbol
   Ⓒ map : community
   Ⓓ road : street

4. What did Allen add to his map?

   Ⓐ a restaurant
   Ⓑ a bank
   Ⓒ a store
   Ⓓ a gas station

5. Allen's map has a legend. The legend

   Ⓐ leads to the river
   Ⓑ shows how to get to Allen's house
   Ⓒ tells a story
   Ⓓ explains the symbols on the map

Winter Carnival

These are new words to practice.

Say each word 10 times.

✳ obstacle   ✳ ticket

✳ course   ✳ plan

✳ guess   ✳ carnival

✳ dart   ✳ quarter

Choose one new word to write.

_____

- -

_____

Winter Carnival

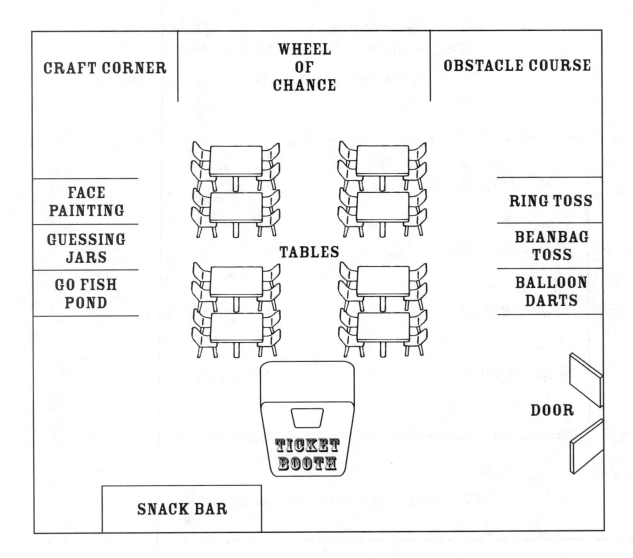

Mona's class is having a winter carnival. Mona helped plan it. She drew a map to show what would be at the carnival.

They will have the carnival in the school gym. They will sell tickets. One ticket will cost a quarter. Each game will take one ticket.

People can buy food. The snack bar will have popcorn and juice. There will be caramel apples.

Mona thinks the carnival will be fun. She will invite her neighbors. They have three children.

Winter Carnival

**Look at the picture on page 115. Read the story.
Use the picture and the story to answer the questions.**

1. A path with things in the way is

   Ⓐ morning and evening

   Ⓑ an obstacle course

   Ⓒ a ladder

   Ⓓ a ring toss

2. Where can Mona catch a prize?

   Ⓐ go fish pond

   Ⓑ ring toss

   Ⓒ craft corner

   Ⓓ balloon darts

3. This story is mainly about

   Ⓐ throwing a beanbag

   Ⓑ having a snack

   Ⓒ making a pond

   Ⓓ planning a carnival

4. Which game is not at the carnival?

   Ⓐ beanbag toss

   Ⓑ hopscotch

   Ⓒ balloon darts

   Ⓓ go fish pond

5. Think about how the word *fish* relates to *pond*. Which words relate in the same way?

   > **fish : pond**

   Ⓐ chan : guess

   Ⓑ popcorn : bag

   Ⓒ ticket : snack

   Ⓓ plan : map

The Best Field Trip

These are new words to practice.
Say each word 10 times.

✳ environment   ✳ wing

✳ museum   ✳ planetarium

✳ exhibit   ✳ explore

✳ hall   ✳ display

Choose one new word to write.

_____

– –

_____

The Best Field Trip

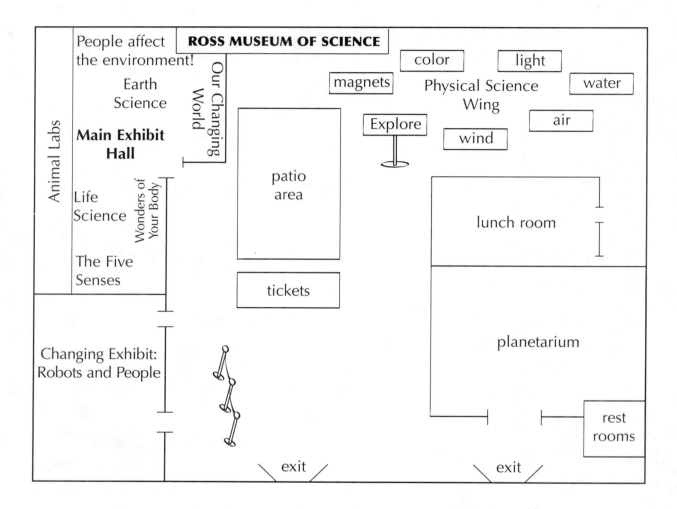

Simon's class went on a field trip. They went to the science museum. Each group got a map of the museum.

Simon wanted to see the new exhibit. He saw a robot on display. He watched the robot move. He learned about many kinds of robots.

After lunch Simon's group went to the Physical Science Wing. They had fun playing with sailboats. They made paper airplanes. Simon flew his plane in the wind tunnel.

Simon's class had to go back to school. Simon was sad to leave the museum. He hoped he could come again soon.

The Best Field Trip

**Look at the picture on page 118. Read the story.
Use the picture and the story to answer the questions.**

1. This month's changing *exhibit* is about

   Ⓐ cars
   Ⓑ money
   Ⓒ robots
   Ⓓ computers

2. This story is mainly about

   Ⓐ how to see animals
   Ⓑ how to find your way around the museum
   Ⓒ how to change Earth
   Ⓓ how to explore

3. What did Simon see at the museum?

   Ⓐ art displays
   Ⓑ history displays
   Ⓒ science displays
   Ⓓ sports displays

4. Think about how the word *wing* relates to *museum*. Which words relate in the same way?

   wing : museum

   Ⓐ finger : hand
   Ⓑ Earth : planet
   Ⓒ exhibit : model
   Ⓓ robot : person

5. The Physical Science Wing is

   Ⓐ the part that makes the building fly
   Ⓑ where you can see birds
   Ⓒ where you will see planets
   Ⓓ another part of the museum

Field Day

These are new words to practice.
Say each word 10 times.

* arena   * stand

* soccer   * goal

* referee   * bleacher

* concession   * park

Choose one new word to write.

_____

- -

_____

Field Day

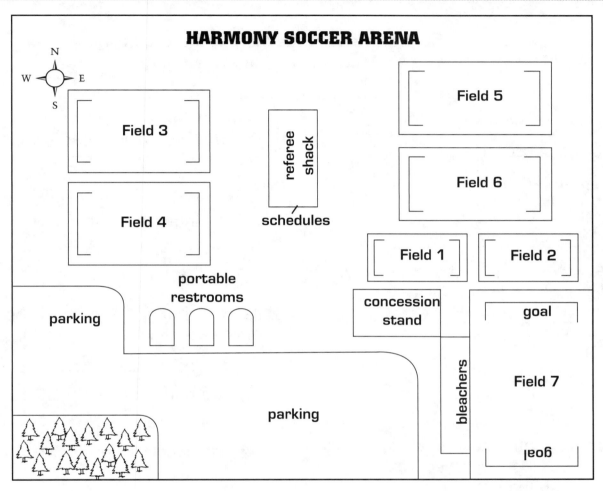

Today Jamal will go to a field day. Many soccer teams will play. Jamal's team will play three or four other teams. One team will win the final game. That team will be the champions.

Jamal plays goalie. He stands in the goal box. He blocks the goals the other team tries to make. He throws the ball back to his teammates.

Jamal gets a map of the soccer arena. He checks the schedule. His team will play its first game in 30 minutes. They will play on Field 6. Jamal goes to Field 6. His coach is there ready to talk with the team and practice drills.

Jamal will enjoy the field day. He will play soccer and see his friends. He hopes his team will do well.

Field Day

**Look at the picture on page 121. Read the story.
Use the picture and the story to answer the questions.**

1. This story is mainly about

   Ⓐ a soccer arena

   Ⓑ a parking lot

   Ⓒ a goal

   Ⓓ a football

2. Someone who makes sure players follow the rules is called a

   Ⓐ goalie

   Ⓑ coach

   Ⓒ referee

   Ⓓ parent

3. Think about how the word *soccer* relates to *goal.* Which words relate in the same way?

soccer : goal

   Ⓐ field : bleachers

   Ⓑ football : touchdown

   Ⓒ concession : food

   Ⓓ stand : shack

4. Jamal wants to know when his friend plays. Where can he find a schedule?

   Ⓐ at the concession stand

   Ⓑ on the referee shack

   Ⓒ from another player

   Ⓓ at Field 4

5. Jamal is hungry. Where will he most likely find food?

   Ⓐ the concession stand

   Ⓑ the parking lot

   Ⓒ the referee shack

   Ⓓ the soccer field

Silly Sentences

These are new words to practice.
Say each word 10 times.

✳ deck	✳ turn
✳ object	✳ complete
✳ article	✳ set
✳ stack	✳ shuffle

Choose one new word to write.

_____

- -

_____

Silly Sentences

Players

4 to 6 people

Object

Use word cards to make a complete sentence.

Things you need

one deck of word cards*

> * The deck has noun, verb, and adjective cards. One card has the word *the*, one card has the word *a*, and one card has the word *an*. These words are articles.

paper

pencils

How to play

Place cards facedown in a stack. Set the three article cards faceup for all players to use. Players take turns taking one card at a time from the deck. Players receive five points for each complete sentence.

Sentences may sound silly, but they must be complete. When someone makes a sentence, shuffle the cards. Repeat the game.

Mr. Jansen put the class in groups. He gave each group a deck of word cards.

Alyssa found the cards with the words *the, a,* and *an*. She placed these faceup on the table. Everyone could use these cards.

Joel was the first person to make a complete sentence. Joel wrote his sentence on a piece of paper. He received five points.

Joel took all the cards. He shuffled them and placed them facedown. Everyone took turns taking cards again.

Silly Sentences

Read the directions on page 124. Read the story.
Use the directions and the story to answer the questions.

1. Where did Alyssa put the deck of cards?

   Ⓐ in a box under the table

   Ⓑ in her hand

   Ⓒ in a stack facedown

   Ⓓ on the floor by her desk

2. This story is mainly about

   Ⓐ a deck of cards

   Ⓑ a game with words

   Ⓒ a silly joke

   Ⓓ a class party

3. Alyssa could win the game by

   Ⓐ making a sentence

   Ⓑ getting all the cards

   Ⓒ getting the most points

   Ⓓ giving her cards to someone

4. Think about how the word *cards* relates to *deck*. Which words relate in the same way?

cards : deck

   Ⓐ words : sentence

   Ⓑ points : win

   Ⓒ players : turn

   Ⓓ paper : pencil

5. The *object* of a game is

   Ⓐ something you eat

   Ⓑ something you take

   Ⓒ what you use to play

   Ⓓ what you try to do

Build Your Own Team

These are new words to practice.
Say each word 10 times.

* form   * remain

* position   * ask

* follow   * count

* deal   * umpire

Choose one new word to write.

_____

- -

_____

Build Your Own Team

Players

4 to 6 people

Object

Form a baseball team.

Things you need

deck of game cards

How to play

The deck has 56 cards. There are six cards of each position as follows:

- pitcher
- catcher
- first base
- second base
- third base
- shortstop
- left field
- center field
- right field

The deck has one umpire and one coach card.

Deal six cards to each player. Place the remaining cards facedown. The first player may take a card from the stack or ask for a card from another player's hand.

The umpire and coach cards do not count as part of a team. A player does not want to get these cards. The first player who has one card for each position wins.

Martin plays a game with his friends: Conner, Scott, and Devon. Martin deals six cards to each person.

Conner takes the first turn. He looks at his cards. He still needs shortstop, center field, and right field. He takes a card from Martin.

Conner got Martin's coach card. Then Martin takes a card from the stack.

The four boys play until Martin wins. Martin has one card for each position. He has a baseball team!

Build Your Own Team

**Look at the directions on page 127. Read the story.
Use the directions and the story to answer the questions.**

1. When Martin *deals* the cards,

   (A) he agrees to play the game

   (B) he gives each player a card

   (C) he plays baseball

   (D) he takes all the cards

2. How many cards will the winner have in his hand?

   (A) 9

   (B) 6

   (C) 56

   (D) 4

3. This story is mainly about

   (A) a sports card collection

   (B) a new coach

   (C) a baseball game

   (D) a card game

4. Think about how the word *umpire* relates to *baseball*. Which words relate in the same way?

   umpire : baseball

   (A) player : position

   (B) group : team

   (C) referee : basketball

   (D) deal : take

5. Why isn't the umpire part of the team?

   (A) he doesn't like baseball

   (B) he makes sure players follow the rules

   (C) he watches the game

   (D) he doesn't know how to play

The Race Is On!

These are new words to practice.
Say each word 10 times.

✳ equipment	✳ select
✳ traffic	✳ allow
✳ piece	✳ forward
✳ finish	✳ space

Choose one new word to write.

_____

- - - - - - - - - - - - - - - - - -

_____

The Race Is On!

Players

4 to 6 people

Object

To reach the finish line first

Equipment

traffic cards

game pieces

game board

How to play

Place game pieces on Start. Place traffic cards facedown on the traffic light picture.

The first player takes a traffic card from the stack. A green card allows the player to move forward the number of spaces shown. A red card means the player must move back the number of spaces shown. Yellow cards tell the player to do something. The player does not move his or her piece.

Gary plays a game with Timothy and Manuel. They each select a game piece. Gary has a green van, Timothy has a blue truck, and Manuel has a red car.

Timothy takes a traffic card. It has a green dot and a number four on it. He moves forward four spaces.

Manuel's card has a yellow dot. The card says Manuel should jump in place three times. Manuel jumps three times, but he does not get to move his car.

The boys take turns. They take cards and move their game pieces. Soon Gary's green van crosses the finish line. He is the winner.

The Race Is On!

**Look at the directions on page 130. Read the story.
Use the directions and the story to answer the questions.**

1. Manuel had a yellow card. He could

   Ⓐ move his car forward

   Ⓑ move his car back

   Ⓒ not move his car at all

   Ⓓ hop five times

2. This story is mainly about

   Ⓐ a running game

   Ⓑ a racing game

   Ⓒ a colors game

   Ⓓ a puzzle

3. Why did Timothy move forward four spaces?

   Ⓐ he got a yellow card

   Ⓑ he got a red card

   Ⓒ he got a green card

   Ⓓ he got a four on the spinner

4. The *equipment* is

   Ⓐ what you need to play the game

   Ⓑ the tools you need to make the game

   Ⓒ how you win

   Ⓓ where you put your game piece

5. Think about how the word *start* relates to *finish*. Which words relate in the same way?

start : finish

   Ⓐ pieces : board

   Ⓑ red : yellow

   Ⓒ object : win

   Ⓓ forward : back

Grocery Store Race

These are new words to practice.
Say each word 10 times.

* disk
* cursor
* click
* item

* checkout
* grocery
* possible
* deposit

Choose one new word to write.

_____

- -

_____

132

Grocery Store Race

Players

1 person

Setup

1. Insert disk.
2. Move cursor to correct circle and click mouse.

Object

Select items and go to Checkout as fast as possible.

○ start

○ quit

How to play

Each player begins with a set amount of money. Click on the items you would like to buy. When you are finished, go to Checkout. If you spend too much, you need to return something. If you have money left over, you may deposit the money in the bank.

Produce	Dairy	Drinks	Checkout	
$2	$5	$1	you spent	○ Exit
$3	$3	$2	money left	○ Bank
next	next	next	next	○ New Game

Nita has played this computer game before. She wants to play faster this time. Nita saved three dollars in the bank at the end of the last game. She will add that to her money at the start of this game.

Nita selects an apple and a pear. She puts cheese in her basket.

Nita can get a drink or she can save her money. She wants to finish quickly. She clicks on juice.

Nita goes to Checkout. She exits the game. She finishes in four minutes. Nita beat her previous time!

Grocery Store Race

**Look at the directions on page 133. Read the story.
Use the directions and the story to answer the questions.**

1. This story is mainly about

   Ⓐ how to play a computer game

   Ⓑ how to go on a picnic

   Ⓒ how to shop for food

   Ⓓ how to save money

2. When you *click* the mouse button

   Ⓐ you turn on the computer

   Ⓑ you feed the mouse

   Ⓒ you tell the computer to do something

   Ⓓ you go to the store

3. Think about how the word *click* relates to *cursor*. Which words relate in the same way?

click : cursor

   Ⓐ computer : screen

   Ⓑ select : item

   Ⓒ setup : play

   Ⓓ next : exit

4. What can you not do at the end of the game?

   Ⓐ start a new game

   Ⓑ exit the game

   Ⓒ go to the bank

   Ⓓ get more money

5. What happens if you spend too much money?

   Ⓐ you have to borrow more money

   Ⓑ you have to put items back

   Ⓒ you lose the game

   Ⓓ you cannot play again

Bouncing Ball

These are new words to practice.
Say each word 10 times.

✳ playground	✳ once
✳ circle	✳ between
✳ bounce	✳ out
✳ next	✳ directions

Choose one new word to write.

_____

- -

_____

Bouncing Ball

Players

At least 5 people

Object

Try to be one of the last two players.

Equipment

playground ball

How to play

Stand in a circle. The first player bounces the ball once to the person standing next to him or her. When the ball has gone around the circle one time, everyone takes a step back.

Players again bounce the ball to the next person. This time, the ball may bounce twice between people.

Each time the ball goes around the circle once, everyone takes a step back. In each round, the ball may bounce one more time between players.

If a player drops the ball, that person is out. The last two players win the game.

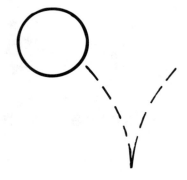

Tory's class has P. E. today. Mr. Swenson gives everyone the directions to a game. They read the directions in health class before P. E. class.

The class stands in a large circle. Stephen stands next to Tory. When Tory gets the ball, she bounces it to Stephen. He bounces it to Mr. Swenson.

Everyone takes a step back. This time Tory bounces the ball two times. She hopes she can stay in the game a long time.

Bouncing Ball

**Look at the directions on page 136. Read the story.
Use the directions and the story to answer the questions.**

1. What happens when someone drops the ball?

    Ⓐ that person tries again

    Ⓑ that person wins

    Ⓒ that person is out

    Ⓓ that person steps closer

2. This story is mainly about

    Ⓐ a game where you run

    Ⓑ a game with a ball

    Ⓒ a game where you hit a ball

    Ⓓ a game in the water

3. What did Tory do first?

    Ⓐ bounce the ball

    Ⓑ stand in a circle

    Ⓒ read the directions

    Ⓓ step back

4. When you *bounce* a ball

    Ⓐ you hit the ball with a stick

    Ⓑ it hits the ground and comes back up

    Ⓒ you put it on a spring

    Ⓓ you throw it away from you

5. Think about how the word *first* relates to *last*. Which words relate in the same way?

first : last

    Ⓐ in : out

    Ⓑ bounce : ball

    Ⓒ skip : step

    Ⓓ once : twice

Space Challenge

These are new words to practice.
Say each word 10 times.

* pry
* obstacle
* northern
* warning

* whirlwind
* distant
* challenge
* overcome

Choose one new word to write.

_____

- -

_____

Space Challenge

Setup

1. Turn on TV and control box.

2. Move control pad to select game.

Object

Get back to Earth

Characters

Pent

A look up answers

B use pencil to write, poke, or pry open

Pent is smart. He can read and take notes.

Special: Pent's pencil can be used as a tool to fix things.

Zoom

A quickly move around ship

B drive ship

Zoom has fast feet and hands to work spaceship controls.

Special: Zoom's quick speed will help you escape from trouble.

Playing the game

Direct your spaceship toward Earth. Your ship may stop at planets or other obstacles. A warning sign will flash to state a challenge. Use tools to overcome obstacles.

Pent and Zoom were in their backyard. They were watching the northern lights. A huge whirlwind sucked them into outer space.

They landed on a distant planet. Now they are trying to get back to Earth. At each place Pent and Zoom stop, they face new challenges. Help them overcome obstacles and get back to Earth.

Space Challenge

**Read the directions on page 139. Read the story.
Use the directions and the story to answer the questions.**

1. Pent and Zoom will face many *challenges.* They will deal with

    (A) things that are fun to do

    (B) things they are not able to do

    (C) things they think are wrong

    (D) things that are hard and require extra work

2. How can Pent and Zoom get back to Earth? They must

    (A) overcome obstacles

    (B) read a book

    (C) visit every planet

    (D) wear a space suit

3. This story is mainly about

    (A) writing notes

    (B) fixing a broken ship

    (C) getting lost on Earth

    (D) playing a video game

4. Think about how the word *move* relates to *stop.* Which words relate in the same way?

    | move : stop |

    (A) look : write

    (B) fast : quick

    (C) left : right

    (D) space : planet

5. What helps Pent and Zoom escape trouble?

    (A) Pent's pencil

    (B) Zoom's quick speed

    (C) staying inside at night

    (D) the northern lights

Answer Sheets

Student Name:

_____

Title of Reading Passage:

_____

1. (a) (b) (c) (d)
2. (a) (b) (c) (d)
3. (a) (b) (c) (d)
4. (a) (b) (c) (d)
5. (a) (b) (c) (d)

Student Name:

_____

Title of Reading Passage:

_____

1. (a) (b) (c) (d)
2. (a) (b) (c) (d)
3. (a) (b) (c) (d)
4. (a) (b) (c) (d)
5. (a) (b) (c) (d)

Student Name:

_____

Title of Reading Passage:

_____

1. (a) (b) (c) (d)
2. (a) (b) (c) (d)
3. (a) (b) (c) (d)
4. (a) (b) (c) (d)
5. (a) (b) (c) (d)

Student Name:

_____

Title of Reading Passage:

_____

1. (a) (b) (c) (d)
2. (a) (b) (c) (d)
3. (a) (b) (c) (d)
4. (a) (b) (c) (d)
5. (a) (b) (c) (d)

Vocabulary List

across
add
adjective
after
aisle
allow
alphabetical
apostrophe
arcade
arena
arrive
article
ask
attraction
backpack
balance
bandage
barbecue
bare
batter
beach
begin
between
biography
bleacher
bold
bounce
bridge
calendar
calorie
candle
caption
car pool
careful
carnival
cartoons
catalog
catch
challenge
champion
channel
chart
checkout
chef
cinema
circle
click
climate
clinic
closed
coach
college
community
compass rose
complete
compound
concession
conclusion
connect
conserve
contraction
corn
corner
cotton
count

course
cover
crab
cranberry
create
cursor
custom
dart
deal
deck
decoration
definition
demonstration
depart
deposit
desired
dictionary
diet
directions
disk
display
distant
drawer
drop
each
edge
electrical
end
energy
enough
enter
entertainment
environment
equipment
eraser
essay
event
example
exercise
exhibit
explore
exposed
extra
fact
fat
fee
festival
fiction
final
finish
first aid
fix
flat
floor
fold
follow
form
forward
free
fund
future
glitter
glue
goal
grandchild

grocery
guess
guide
half
hall
hang
Hanukkah
heading
health
hoe
hoop
host
hotel
hypothesis
include
information
ingredients
instructions
interview
invitation
item
job
Kwanzaa
lab
label
landform
lead
leader
legend
lengthwise
lesson
lettuce
library
light
limit
lip balm
liquid
listen
llama
loose
magazine
map
mark
marker
material
matinee
maximum
meaning
measure
medicine
meet
model
moment
muffin
museum
mute
nearly
news
next
nonfiction
northern
notebook
notes
noun
object

observe
obstacle
ointment
once
opposite
order
out
overcome
pack
park
participate
party
peas
people
pepperoni
perfect
piano
picture
piece
plan
planetarium
playground
position
possible
power
practice
press
preview
print
procedure
produce
project
provide
pry
quality
quarter
question
racquetball
rake
ranger
record
records
referee
reference
regular
remain
remember
remind
remote control
reserve
resource
restroom
review
road
rock
ruler
salad
salute
sand
scale
schedule
season
seize
select
set

shampoo
shot
shuffle
shuttle
sift
site
snack
soccer
sole
soon
sound
space
species
splash
stack
stand
study
sunglasses
supply
symbol
taco
teaspoon
terminal
text
textbook
theater
theme
ticket
tide
token
tomorrow
toothpaste
top
topic
topping
tortilla
tournament
towel
traffic
trail
treadmill
triangle
trowel
turn
tutor
umpire
unpack
usually
VCR
vegetable
vehicle
verb
wait
warning
waste
weights
welcome
which
whirlwind
wing
wrap

Answer Key

Page 11—Shopping for Dinner
1. B
2. A
3. D
4. A
5. C

Page 14—Going to the Library
1. B
2. A
3. D
4. C
5. A

Page 17—Pizza Party
1. C
2. B
3. C
4. D
5. B

Page 20—Fitness Is Fun
1. B
2. A
3. D
4. C
5. A

Page 23—Going to the Clinic
1. C
2. C
3. B
4. B
5. D

Page 26—Back to School
1. B
2. A
3. C
4. D
5. B

Page 29—Going to the Movies
1. C
2. D
3. A
4. B
5. C

Page 32—Hannah's Science Project
1. A
2. B
3. D
4. A
5. D

Page 35—Helping Grandpa
1. C
2. D
3. A
4. B
5. C

Page 38—Listen Carefully
1. A
2. D
3. C
4. B
5. A

Page 41—Birthday Fun
1. B
2. C
3. A
4. C
5. D

Page 44—Junko Reads Directions
1. C
2. B
3. D
4. B
5. B

Page 47—Wrapping a Gift
1. C
2. D
3. A
4. B
5. C

Page 50—A Special Evening
1. A
2. C
3. C
4. D
5. B

Page 53—Fun in the Garden
1. B
2. D
3. A
4. B
5. D

Page 56—After School Snack
1. A
2. C
3. A
4. C
5. B

Page 59—David Knows How to Clean
1. C
2. C
3. A
4. B
5. D

Page 62—A New House
1. C
2. A
3. B
4. D
5. D

Page 65—Grandma's Kitchen
1. A
2. B
3. C
4. C
5. B

Page 68—Winter Vacation
1. B
2. C
3. A
4. C
5. A

Page 71—Shooting Hoops
1. A
2. B
3. C
4. A
5. D

Page 74—Scout Events
1. C
2. D
3. B
4. B
5. A

Page 77—Lessons for Luke
1. B
2. A
3. C
4. D
5. C

Page 80–Water World
1. A
2. B
3. D
4. C
5. B

Answer Key *(cont.)*

Page 83—Classroom Jobs
1. C
2. B
3. D
4. B
5. D

Page 86—Walking on the Beach
1. B
2. A
3. C
4. A
5. C

Page 89—Reading a Textbook
1. A
2. C
3. B
4. D
5. C

Page 92—Meet a Geographer
1. B
2. A
3. D
4. D
5. B

Page 95—Come to the Science Fair
1. C
2. D
3. A
4. B
5. A

Page 98—Today's News for Today's Kids
1. C
2. B
3. A
4. C
5. D

Page 101—Wonderful Wildcats
1. B
2. A
3. C
4. D
5. B

Page 104—Learning About the Dictionary
1. C
2. D
3. B
4. B
5. A

Page 107—Camping at the Beach
1. A
2. B
3. C
4. D
5. C

Page 110—What's the Weather?
1. D
2. C
3. B
4. B
5. A

Page 113—Making a Map
1. C
2. B
3. A
4. C
5. D

Page 116—Winter Carnival
1. B
2. A
3. D
4. B
5. B

Page 119—The Best Field Trip
1. C
2. B
3. C
4. A
5. D

Page 122—Field Day
1. A
2. C
3. B
4. B
5. A

Page 125—Silly Sentences
1. C
2. B
3. C
4. A
5. D

Page 128—Build Your Own Team
1. B
2. A
3. D
4. C
5. B

Page 131—The Race Is On!
1. C
2. B
3. C
4. A
5. D

Page 134—Grocery Store Race
1. A
2. C
3. B
4. D
5. B

Page 137—Bouncing Ball
1. C
2. B
3. C
4. B
5. A

Page 140—Space Challenge
1. D
2. A
3. D
4. C
5. B